ANNE FRANK'S TALES
FROM THE SECRET ANNEX

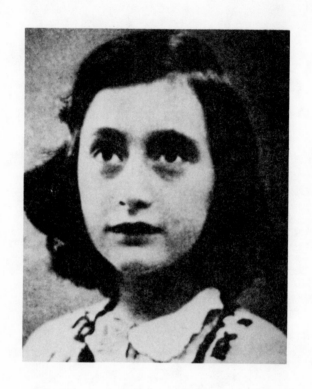

'ANNE FRANK'S TALES FROM THE SECRET ANNEX

With translations by
RALPH MANHEIM
and
MICHEL MOK

DOUBLEDAY & COMPANY, INC.

GARDEN CITY, NEW YORK

1984

The original manuscripts
are in the Anne Frank House in Amsterdam
and in the Institute for War Documentation in Amsterdam.

Portions of this book were previously published in
The Works of Anne Frank (Doubleday, 1959)
and *Tales from the House Behind* (Bantam, 1966).
This volume has been previously published by Pocket Books (1983).

Originally published in Dutch as
*Verhaaltjes en Gebeurtenissen uit het Achterhuis
beschreven door Anne Frank*
Copyright © 1949, 1960 by Otto Frank
Copyright © 1982 by Anne Frank-Fonds, Basel
English translation copyright © 1952, 1959 by Otto H. Frank
English translation copyright © 1983 by Doubleday & Company, Inc.

Library of Congress Cataloging in Publication Data
Frank, Anne, 1929-1945.
Anne Frank's Tales from the Secret Annex.
Translation of:
Verhaaltjes en Gebeurtenissen uit het Achterhuis.
I. Title. II. Title: Tales from the secret annex.
PT5881.16.R26V413   1984   839.3'186209
ISBN: 0-385-18715-7
Library of Congress Catalog Card Number: 82-45871
ALL RIGHTS RESERVED
PRINTED IN THE UNITED STATES OF AMERICA

9 8 7 6 5 4 3 2

CONTENTS

CONTENTS

EDITOR'S NOTE

This edition of *Anne Frank's Tales from the Secret Annex* contains material appearing for the first time in hardcover: "Paula's Plane Trip," "Jackie," "Cady's Life," "The Flea," "The Battle of the Potatoes," "Villains!" "Sunday," and "Who Is Interesting?" These tales, as well as "Roomers or Subtenants," "The Porter's Family," and "The Sink of Iniquity" have been newly translated by Ralph Manheim. The other pieces in this collection have been translated by Michel Mok.

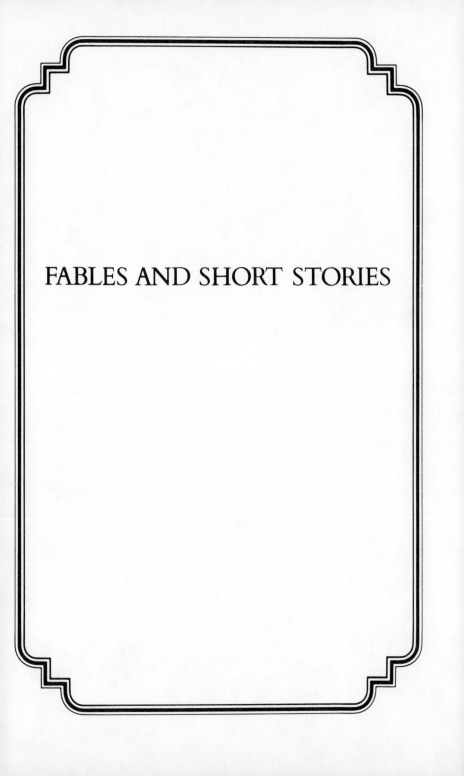

FABLES AND SHORT STORIES

Kitty

Kitty is the girl next door. In fair weather, I can watch her playing in the yard through our window. Kitty has a wine-red velvet frock for Sundays and a cotton one for every day; she has pale-blond hair with tiny braids, and clear blue eyes.

Kitty has a sweet mother, but her father is dead. The mother is a laundress; sometimes she is gone during the day, cleaning other people's houses, and at night she does the wash for her customers.

Often she shakes out carpets late at night and hangs wash on the line. Kitty has six brothers and sisters. The smallest screams a lot and hangs onto the skirts of his eleven-year-old sister when Mother says, "Children, it's bedtime!"

Kitty has a small cat which is so black that it looks like a Moor. She takes good care of the kitten, and every evening, before bedtime, you can hear her call, "Kitty, kitty, kitty!" That's how she came to be called Kitty, which may not be her name at all. She also has two rabbits, a white one and a brown one, that hop up and down in the grass.

Sometimes Kitty is naughty, just like other children. This happens mostly when she quarrels with her brothers. It's a sight to see her fight with them—she beats, kicks, and even bites them, and the little boys respect their sturdy sister.

"There are errands to be done!" Mother calls. Quickly Kitty sticks her fingers in her ears, so that she'll be able to say that she didn't hear her mother. Kitty hates running errands, but she wouldn't lie to escape it; Kitty doesn't lie; you need only to look into her blue eyes to know that.

One of Kitty's brothers is sixteen and works as an office boy. This brother sometimes bosses the other children as if he were their father. Kitty doesn't dare to contradict him, for she knows from experience that he is quick with his fists and also that he doesn't mind standing treat if one obeys him. Peter is generous and Kitty loves sweets.

Sundays, when the bell tolls, Kitty's mother and all the children go to church. Kitty prays for her dear father, who is in heaven, and also for her mother, that she may have a long, long life. After church they all go for a walk. Kitty enjoys this a lot; she is fond of wandering through the park, or, better still, through the zoo. But that happens only in September, when it costs a quarter.* Kitty's birthday is in September, and sometimes she asks for a trip to the zoo as a birthday gift. Other gifts her mother cannot afford.

Often Kitty comforts her mother who, after a day's hard work, weeps in the night. Then Kitty promises her

*The Amsterdam Zoological Society is a membership organization. In the month of September, the public is admitted to the park for twenty-five Dutch cents—Trans.

all the things she, herself, would like to have when she is grown up. Kitty wants so badly to be grown up, to earn money, buy pretty clothes, and treat her sisters to sweets, as Peter does. But before she can do all that, Kitty has to learn a lot and go to school for a long time.

Mother wants Kitty to go to Domestic Science School, but the girl doesn't care for that idea at all. She doesn't want a job in the house of some stuck-up lady. She wants to work in a factory, like those jolly chattering girls she sees passing by the window. In a factory you're never alone, you have company to gossip with. And Kitty loves gossiping. Once in a while she has to stand in the corner in school, because she talks too much.

Just the same, Kitty is fond of her teacher, who is sweet and terribly clever. How difficult it must be to study and get to know so much! But one can get along with less. Kitty's mother always says that a girl doesn't get a husband if she is too clever, and that, Kitty thinks, would be just awful. Later she should like to have dear little children, but not such children as her brothers and sisters. Kitty's children are going to be much prettier and sweeter. They will have curly brown hair instead of that straight flaxen stuff, and they will have no freckles, which Kitty has by the hundreds. Kitty doesn't want as many children as her mother has. Two or three would be enough, but, oh, it is so far, far off . . .

"Kitty!" her mother calls. "Come here. Where have you been, naughty girl? Just sitting there dreaming, I guess. Quick, to bed with you!"

Kitty sighs. To be interrupted just as you are thinking of a glorious future!

The Porter's Family

Saturday, August 7, 1943

Neither in winter nor in summer do the porter's family observe the blackout regulations. It's like peacetime, the days when the light burned so sociably in everyone's apartment and you could see the people all sitting around the dining room table or tea table.

In this respect the porter's family don't seem to care whether it's war or peace; anyway, you can look through the brightly lighted window and see Papa, Mamma, the son, and the daughter sitting around the table.

Mamma simply won't have anything to do with the war; she refuses to make ersatz sauce, she'd rather have none at all, she won't drink ersatz tea, she takes peppermint tea instead, and when there's shooting and she doesn't want to hear it, she has an effective remedy for that too, namely, she goes and sits in the shower stall and plays the loudest jazz music on the gramophone. When the neighbors complain, that doesn't bother her, she just brings them some goodies next day to mollify them. The lady on the third floor, whose daughter is engaged to the son of the house, gets a fat pancake and she actually gives Mrs. Steen, her right-hand neighbor, fifty grams of sugar.

The lady dentist on the second floor rear, who employs her youngest daughter as an assistant, isn't neglected either, but Papa is good and mad at her, because every night of shooting costs him three cigarettes.

Papa and Mamma are alone all day. They take loving care of their five rabbits, who get fatter by the day. They have a cradle to sleep in, a shed to keep off the rain, and a tub for a dinner table. In winter they have a little house with windows and nice big rooms. Their daily menu consists of carrot tops and other delicacies. Papa works a lot in the garden; Mamma in the house. Everything is spic and span. Every week she does the windows front and back, every week the floors, every week the kitchenware, always helped by the fat cleaning woman who has had the same position for years.

Papa hasn't got much work now. At present he's porter for the big business office upstairs, and all he has to do is sleep lightly, so as to listen for possible burglars. Mamma used to clean the whole building with the help of the cleaning woman. But since her only daughter has got married and the other has had her tenth child, she has given it up.

It's Mamma's and Papa's greatest joy when the grandchildren come to see them. The whole time you hear them shouting across the garden: "Grampa, Grandma, look at the rabbits, they're doing such funny things." Then Grampa and Grandma go running over, because grandchildren need to be spoiled, that's their opinion. Grandchildren aren't like one's own children, who should be made to toe the line.

Grampa is working hard for his oldest granddaughter; he's making her a canoe for her birthday. I wish I had that kind of grampa.

Eve's Dream

"Good night, Eve, sleep well."

"Same to you, Mum."

Click went the light and Eve lay in the dark, but only for a few moments, because when she got used to the darkness, she saw that her mother had closed the curtains in such a way that an opening was left through which she could look straight into the face of the moon. The moon stood so quietly in the sky; he didn't move, smiled, and was friendly to everyone.

"If I could only be like that," Eve said softly to herself, "always quiet and kind so that everybody would like me. That would be wonderful."

Eve thought and thought about the difference between the moon and herself, who was still so very small. She finally dozed off, and her thoughts seemed to be transformed into a dream, which Eve remembered so keenly next day that she afterward sometimes wondered whether it had not actually happened.

She stood at the entrance of a big park, looking through the fence and not quite daring to go in. Just as she was about to turn back, a little girl with wings came up to her and said, "Go right ahead, Eve, or don't you know the way?"

"No, I don't," said Eve shyly.

"Well, then I will guide you." And with those words, the smart little elf took Eve's hand.

Eve had walked in several parks with her mother and her grandmother, but a park like this one she had never seen.

She saw a wealth of flowers, trees, fields, every imaginable kind of insect, and small animals such as squirrels and turtles. The elf chatted gaily with her, and Eve had got over her fear enough to ask a question. But the elf stopped her by putting a finger to Eve's lips.

"I will show you and explain everything. After each explanation you may ask questions about things you don't understand, but otherwise you must be silent and not interrupt me. If you do, I shall take you home at once, and then you will know just as little as all the other stupid people.

"Well, now I begin: First of all, here is the rose, the queen of flowers. She is so beautiful and smells so wonderful that it goes to everybody's head, and most of all to her own.

"The rose is lovely, elegant, and fragrant, but if something doesn't please her, she immediately turns her thorns in your direction. She is like a spoiled little girl—very pretty and apparently quite sweet, too, but either touch her, or pay a little attention to somebody else, so that she is no longer the center of interest, and she shows her sharp nails. Her tone of voice becomes catty; she is offended but doesn't want to show it, and so her manners turn stilted and she puts on airs."

"But if all this is so, little elf, how is it that everybody considers the rose the queen of flowers?"

"It is because nearly all people are blinded by surface glitter; there are only a few who would not have voted for the rose if there had been an election. The rose is good-looking and dignified, and, just as in the rest of the world, scarcely anyone asks if there might not be another, outwardly a little plainer, perhaps, but inwardly more noble and gifted, for the role of ruler."

"But you yourself think the rose lovely, don't you, little elf?"

"Indeed, I do, and if she wouldn't always push herself into the foreground, she might be lovable as well. But since, by common consent, she is the flower of flowers, she will always regard herself as more beautiful than she really is, and so long as that is so, she will be full of false pride. I don't care for such creatures."

"Do you think that Lena, too, is full of false pride? She is also beautiful and, because she is rich, she is the head of the class."

"Think for a moment, Eve, and you will have to admit that, if little Marie, for example, had some complaint against Lena, Lena would turn the entire class against Marie. The reason? Simply that Marie is plain and poor. And you, all of you, would accept that false reason, because you know that if you did not, you would fall from Lena's good graces. And that, you think, is as bad as having the headmaster angry at you. You wouldn't be permitted to come to her beautiful home, and so you let her boss you. Later in life, such girls as Lena will stand alone, for the others, as they grow older, will understand how wrong she was. Rather than be lonely forever, girls like Lena should change their ways."

"Do you think, then, elf, that I should try to convince the other girls not to listen to Lena?"

"Yes. First she will be furious at you. But later, as she gets more sense and realizes how badly she has acted, she will be grateful and have friends who are more sincere than those she has had until now . . ."

"I understand. But tell me, little elf, am I as full of false pride as the rose?"

"Listen, Eve: people and children who ask themselves such questions prove by that very act that they are free from false pride. You can best answer the question yourself, and I advise you to do so . . . Now let us go on. Look at this: don't you think it is attractive?"

The elf knelt down by a small, blue, bell-shaped flower that waved back and forth in the grass to the rhythm of the wind.

"This little bell is kind, sweet, and simple. It brings joy to the world; it tolls for the other flowers just as a church bell tolls for people. It helps many flowers and comforts them. The little bell is never lonesome; it has music in its small heart. This flower is much happier than the rose. It doesn't care about the praise of others. The rose lives only for and by admiration: if she doesn't get this, she has no other reason to be glad. Her outward splendor is for others; inside she is empty and, therefore, without happiness.

"The little bell, on the other hand, is not exactly beautiful, but it has genuine friends, who value its melodies; those friends live in its flower-heart."

"But the little bell is a pretty flower, too, isn't it?"

"Yes, but not as obviously as the rose. Unfortunately, it is this kind of 'show' that attracts most people."

"But I, too, often feel quite alone and like to have people about me. Is that not good?"

"That has nothing to do with it, Eve. Later, when you grow up, you, too, will hear the song in your heart; I am sure of it."

"Please, dear elf, go on with your story."

"All right, I will go on." The elf pointed upward with her small fingers. Eve looked at a huge, stately chestnut tree.

"This tree is impressive, isn't it?" asked the elf.

"Yes, it is grand; how old do you think it is?"

"It is surely more than a hundred and fifty years old, but it is still straight and doesn't feel old at all. Everybody admires this chestnut for its strength, and he proves that he knows his strength with his indifference about all this admiration. He doesn't tolerate anyone above himself and is egotistical in everything. So long as he lives, nothing else is of any importance. He looks as though he were generous and a support to others. But if you think that, you are mistaken. The chestnut is pleased when no one comes to him with troubles or complaints. He has a good life, but he begrudges it to everyone else. The trees and flowers know this. When they are in trouble, they go to the sympathetic pine and forget about the chestnut.

"Still, the chestnut, too, has a very small song in that big heart of his; you can tell that by his liking for the birds. For them he always has a little spot, and he often gives them a little something, though not much."

"Can the chestnut tree also be compared to some kind of person?"

"That, too, you need not ask, Eve. All living beings can be compared with each other, and the chestnut is no exception. He is not bad, you know, but neither is he good. He doesn't do anyone harm, lives his own life, and is satisfied. Any other questions, Eve?"

"No, I understand everything, and I am very grateful to you for your explanations, dear elf. Now I am going home. Will you come again sometime to tell me more?"

"That is not possible. Sleep well, Eve."

The elf was gone. Eve woke up; the sun had replaced the moon, and a cuckoo clock at the neighbors' called out seven.

The dream had made a big impression on Eve. Nearly every day she caught herself doing or saying little unpleasant things, which she then corrected at once according to the elf's good advice. She also tried hard not always to give in to Lena. But girls like that feel at once that someone is making an effort to "take them down a peg or two." She defended herself vigorously, especially when Eve proposed some game in which another girl would be the leader. Then Lena did everything she could to turn her faithful following against Eve.

Eve noticed with pleasure that Lena wasn't quite as smart in her dealings with her as she was with little Marie. As Marie was a small, slight, and shy girl, it amazed Eve that she dared to stand up against Lena. As she got to know her better, it became very clear to Eve that Marie, as a friend, was to be valued much above Lena.

Eve had told her mother nothing about the elf. She hardly knew why. Until now, she had confided in her mother, but for the first time she felt the need to keep something to herself. She didn't understand it, but she had a feeling that Mummy wouldn't be quite "with her" in this.

The little elf was so lovely, and Mummy had not been in the big park and hadn't seen the elf. Eve couldn't describe the elf's appearance. It wasn't long before the dream had such an influence on Eve that her mother noticed the change in her daughter. She talked about more interesting things than before and didn't get excited about trifles. But since Eve didn't speak of what had brought about the change, the mother didn't want to force herself into the child's confidence.

And so Eve lived on, thinking always of the elf's good counsel. She never saw the elf again. Lena no longer was the head of the class. The other girls now led the group by turns. At first, this had made Lena very cross, but when she found that angry words didn't help, she began to behave in a more friendly manner. Finally, her classmates, finding that she had outgrown her old faults, treated her like everyone else.

Eve decided to tell her mother of her experience. To her surprise, Mummy didn't laugh, but said: "That was a great privilege the elf gave you, Eve. I don't believe that she would think many children fit to receive it. Think always of the elf's trust in you, and don't talk about it to anyone. Do always what the elf told you, and don't get away from the path she showed you."

As Eve grew older, she became known for her good deeds. When she was sixteen, everyone in the community prized her as a kind, gentle, and helpful girl. Every time she did something good she felt warm and glad inside, and slowly she began to understand what the elf had meant by "the song in her heart."

When she was grown up, the solution of the dream and who and what the elf had been suddenly came to her one day. She knew, as if in a flash, that it had been her own conscience which, in her dream, had shown her what was right. She was deeply thankful that, in her childhood, she had had the little elf as a guide and example.

Long ago, when I was little, Pim used to tell me stories about "naughty Paula"; he had a whole collection of stories and I was crazy about them. And now again, when I'm with Pim at night, he sometimes tells me about Paula, and I've written down the latest story:

Paula's Plane Trip

Wednesday, December 22, 1943

CHAPTER I

Paula had wanted for a long time to see the inside of an aeroplane. Her father had been working lately at an airfield near Berlin, where Paula and her mother were also living.

One fine day, when things were fairly quiet at the airfield, she took her courage in both hands and climbed into the first plane that came her way. As calmly as can be, she looked into every nook and corner, and finally stopped to inspect the cockpit. She was just going to let herself out when to her indescribable horror she heard loud voices outside. Quickly she crawled under one of the benches and waited trembling to see what would happen.

The voices came closer and closer, and a moment later she saw two men step into the plane; they went all over and almost bumped into the bench under which she was lying. They sat down together on a bench behind her and started talking in a dialect that Paula couldn't understand at all. After ten or fifteen minutes they stood up, and one of them got out, but the other shut himself up in the pilot's cabin for a while and came back dressed as a pilot. Then the second came back, followed by six other men, who all got into the plane, and, trembling, Paula heard the engine starting and the propellers beginning to turn.

CHAPTER 2

Since in spite of her boldness, she was sometimes scary and fainthearted and sometimes unexpectedly brave, there was no way of knowing which of these two contrasts would now take over.

As it happened, she was now uncommonly brave, and when they had been flying for a while, she suddenly came out from under the bench. To the boundless amazement of the crew, she introduced herself and told them how she had got there.

What was to be done with Paula? The crew talked it over and decided that they had no other choice than to keep her with them. She heard them say they were flying to Russia to bomb the Russian lines.

With a sigh, she lay down on a bench and fell asleep. *Bim bam boom* . . . suddenly Paula sat up straight and stared at the men out of wide-open eyes. But nobody had time to bother with her, because the Russians were shooting at the enemy plane for all they were worth. All of a sudden, Paula screamed, the benches trembled, the windows crashed, and a couple of shells fell inside the plane, a dive bomber, and the plane went down for a crash landing.

Some Russians came running and put the whole crew in handcuffs. You can imagine the funny look on these foreigners' faces when they suddenly saw a little girl of about thirteen standing in front of them. The Germans and Russians didn't understand a word of each other's language, so a young Russian took Paula by the hand and they followed the crew to a prison camp. The head of the camp laughed heartily at the sight of Paula standing there so unafraid. He didn't want to take this little girl prisoner along with the others, so he decided that he'd look around next day behind the front and see if he could find some simple people to take the little girl in until the war was over.

CHAPTER 3

One rainy morning after she had spent about a week in the commander's office, Paula was led out just as she was and put in a big truck that was taking wounded soldiers to the hospital. For five hours the truck rattled and bumped over the cobblestones, while outside a curtain of rain cut off the view. The loneliness of the road was relieved by a house here and there, but all those houses seemed dead. At the start of the trip, the roaring of cannon could still be heard in the distance, then it got gradually fainter, and in the end it stopped altogether.

Suddenly the road got busier, they passed a few cars, and then the truck stopped outside a white house, painted from top to bottom with red crosses. The wounded men were carried inside, where they were taken in hand by friendly nurses.

When they were all out, the driver went on without a

word. Another whole hour passed, then he stopped again and Paula saw a fairly large farmhouse between the trees. The driver pointed in the direction of the house, and Paula understood that she was to get out. She stood on the road waiting for the driver, but before she knew what was happening, the truck disappeared and she was alone on the deserted road. She thought to herself: "What funny people the Russians are! Here in this foreign country they just leave me to my fate. I bet the Germans wouldn't do that!" (You must bear in mind that Paula was a German girl.) But then she remembered that the driver had pointed in the direction of the house. So she crossed the road, opened the gate, and found herself in a kind of fenced-in meadow. In front of the house she saw a woman who was working and a little girl who was hanging up washing.

Holding out her hand, Paula went up to the woman. All she said was: "Paula Müller." The woman also held out her hand after wiping it on her soaking-wet apron, and said: "Yustichiyarreya kolovnya." Paula thought that was her name, but it just meant: "Welcome here."

CHAPTER 4

Mrs. Kantavoska (that was the woman's name) lived on that farm with her husband and three children. She also had a hired man and two maids. Three days earlier, she had received word that a girl of about thirteen would probably be arriving in the next few days. And in that case nobody else would be billeted in her house.

That suited Mrs. Kantavoska perfectly, and now she felt sure that this was the girl in question. It was hard for the Kantavoskas to tell Paula what to do. Try as she might, she didn't understand what they wanted of her. For the first two weeks she had difficulty in getting the food down, but since hunger is the best sauce, she soon got used to it, and believe it or not she began to help with the washing and sewing by copying the others.

So Paula stayed on, and when six months had passed she understood Russian fairly well. At the end of another six months, she understood almost everything, and though it wasn't easy for her she even opened her mouth now and then. The Kantavoskas didn't notice any of Paula's naughtiness, she was much too clever for that; and besides, she didn't want to mess up her life there. She did her work, and since she really wasn't as clumsy as she always pretended to be at home, she gradually became a member of the family.

CHAPTER 5

Two years after her arrival at the Kantavoskas, Paula was asked if she'd like to learn reading and writing. She accepted eagerly and from then on she went to reading and writing school three times a week with a girl from the neighborhood. She made quick progress and in twelve weeks she was able to read Russian. Along with the neighbor girl, she also learned dancing, and it wasn't long before she could be seen dancing polkas and mazurkas at cafés for a few cents an evening. She gave half the money she made to Mother Kantavoska and kept the other half, because she had long been thinking up a way of getting out of that country.

CHAPTER 6

She was now sixteen, she hadn't learned much and to Western ways of thinking she might have seemed pretty stupid. So she worked hard at her dancing and it wasn't

long before she had saved money enough to pay for a
ticket from Minsk (that was the district she was in) to
Warsaw. "Once I'm in Warsaw," she thought, "the Red
Cross is sure to send me the rest of the way."

No sooner said than done. One morning when she was
supposed to be going to school, she packed her accumu-
lated belongings in a bag and slipped away.

As she had foreseen, it was no joke walking from the
Kantavoskas' farm to Minsk. A truck driver did give her a
few hours' lift, but the rest of the way she walked, and it
took hours and hours.

When she reached Minsk dead tired later in the afternoon, she went straight to the railroad station and in-
quired about connections with Warsaw. To her horror she
heard that the first train wouldn't be leaving until twelve
the next day. She pleaded to see the stationmaster, and
when he appeared she begged his permission to spend the
night in the waiting room. Permission was granted and she
was so tired she fell asleep in next to no time. When morning came, she woke up stiff in every limb and asked in
bewilderment where she was. But consciousness returned
only too soon, because the grumbling of her stomach
couldn't be ignored. This was a problem Paula hadn't expected. There was a nice waitress at the station buffet and
after hearing Paula's true story she gave her a genuine
Russian bun. She spent the whole morning chatting with
the waitress, and at twelve o'clock, fully revived and in
the best of spirits, she boarded the Warsaw train.

CHAPTER 7

When she got there, the stationmaster told her the way and she went straight to the house of the Red Cross nurses. She stayed longer than she had expected, because none of the nurses knew what to do with her. They had no addresses or anything of organizations that looked for people, and since Paula didn't have a red cent, the nurses could neither put her on a train nor let her starve. In the end, however, they decided they'd just have to buy Miss X a ticket to Berlin, because Paula had told them that once she was in Berlin she'd have no trouble finding her way home.

Paula's parting with the nurses was affectionate and then she took the train again. At the next station a nice young man got in, who soon struck up a conversation with the bold-looking girl. All through the trip Paula could be seen in the company of the handsome young soldier, and when they left the train in Berlin they arranged to meet each other soon.

Paula started out at once and soon reached the house of her parents, but everything was empty and deserted. It had never entered her head that her parents might have moved in the meantime. What was she to do? Again she went to the Red Cross and told them her story in her broken German. Again she was taken in and fed, but was only allowed to stay there for two weeks.

The only news she had of her parents was that her mother had left Berlin to look for work somewhere else and that her father had been drafted in the last year of the war and was lying wounded in some hospital.

Quickly she went looking for a job as a housemaid, and

when she had found one she met Erik, the handsome young man, who found her an engagement in a cabaret three evenings a week. So the Russian dances came in handy again.

CHAPTER 8

Paula had been dancing for quite some time when one evening in the cabaret it was announced that in two weeks' time a big dance recital would be given for the benefit of convalescent soldiers who had recently been discharged from various hospitals. Paula was given a big part in this affair. She had to practice a lot, and when she came home late at night she was so tired she could hardly drag herself out of bed at seven o'clock in the morning. Her only consolation was Erik. Their friendship had grown stronger and deeper, and Paula would really not have known what to do without him. When the big night came, Paula had stage fright for the first time in her life. It seemed so odd having to dance just for men. But she had no choice, the opportunity was too good to be missed, mainly because now she'd have a little more money.

The show went off well and as soon as it was over Paula went straight to the hall to be with Erik. All of a sudden she stopped in her tracks, because right there in front of her stood her own father, talking with another soldier. With a cry of joy, she ran over to him and threw her arms around him.

Her father, who had grown old in the meantime, looked up. He was completely flabbergasted, because he didn't recognize his daughter, either on the stage or now. She actually had to introduce herself.

CHAPTER 9

A week later Paula could be seen walking into the station at Frankfurt on the Main, arm in arm with her father. They were welcomed by Paula's deeply moved mother, who all that time had been hoping in vain for her daughter's return.

When she had told her mother the whole story, her father asked her jokingly if she'd care to get into "that plane over there" and fly back to Russia.

The reader needs to know that this story took place during the war of 1914–18, when the Germans were victorious in their Russian campaign.

Kathy

Kathy sat on the big boulder that lay in the sun in front of the farm. She was thinking, thinking very hard. Kathy was one of those quiet girls. What the youngster in the dirndl apron was thinking about, she alone knew; she never told her thoughts to anyone—she was much too withdrawn for that. She had no friends and probably would have found it hard to get any. Her mother found her a strange child, and the pity of it was that Kathy felt that. Her father, the farmer, was much too busy to concern himself with his only little daughter. And so Kathy was always by herself. It didn't disturb her; she didn't know any better and was soon satisfied.

But on this warm summer evening she sighed deeply as she looked up and glanced at the cornfields. How jolly it would be to play with those girls over there. Look, they ran about, and laughed; what fun they were having! Now the children came closer, and still closer—would they come to her? Oh, how awful, they came—but to laugh at her. She clearly heard them mention her name, not her real name, but the nickname that she hated so much and that she often heard the children whisper—Crazykate!

Oh, how miserable she felt; if she could only run into the house, but if she did, the children would laugh at her all the more. Poor girl, it surely isn't the first time that you have felt so forsaken and envied to other youngsters . . .

"Kathy! Kathy, come home! We are having supper!" Another sigh, and the child slowly rose to obey her mother.

"My, what a cheerful face! We surely have a happy daughter!" the farmer's wife cried when the child, more slowly and more depressed than ever, entered the room. "Can't you say something for yourself?" scolded the woman. Her tone was more unfriendly than she herself knew; her daughter never had been the bright, lively girl she had always wanted.

"Yes, Mother," whispered the child.

"You're a fine one, staying away all morning and not doing a stroke of work. Where have you been?"

"Outside." Kathy felt as though she had a gag in her throat, but the mother misunderstood the girl's embarrassment and now really became curious where the child had been all morning. Again she asked:

"Answer me properly; I want to know where you have been, do you understand? I can't stand that everlasting, slow-witted, crazy behavior!"

At the word that reminded her of the detested nickname, Kathy lost control of herself and burst into tears.

"What is the matter now? You're a real coward! Can't

you tell me where you've been hanging out? Or is that perhaps a big secret?"

The child could not possibly answer; violent sobs kept her from speaking. Suddenly, she upset a chair, ran weeping out of the room and up to the attic, where she sank down on some bags in a corner, sobbing as if her heart would break.

The mother shrugged her shoulders as she cleared the table downstairs; she wasn't surprised at her child's conduct. Such "crazy" moods were not unusual; she decided to let the girl alone—there was nothing to be gained, and the everlasting tears were always on the point of coming. A fine specimen of a twelve-year-old farmer's daughter!

In the attic, Kathy had calmed down somewhat and was collecting her thoughts. She would presently go downstairs, tell her mother that she had simply been sitting on the boulder by the door and thinking about things, and offer to finish all of the work that afternoon. Her mother then would surely understand that she did not mind the work, and should she be asked why she had been sitting still all morning, she would answer that there was something important she HAD to figure out. Then, in the evening, when she had to deliver the eggs, she would buy a pretty, silver, glittering thimble for her mother; she had just enough money to buy one in the village.

Mother would realize that she wasn't so slow-witted and crazy, after all. Oh, if she could only get rid of that dreadful nickname! Here was a thought: If she had any money left over after buying the thimble, she'd get a bag of sweets and, on her way to school, divide them among the girls. Then they'd like her and ask her to play with them. They would soon see that she was as good at games as anyone, and nobody would ever call her anything but Kathy after that.

Softly she descended the stairs. When she met her mother in the passage, all courage to talk and explain the morning's absence left her, and she quickly started cleaning the windows, one of her regular tasks.

It was almost sundown when Kathy took the basket of eggs and began her rounds. After a half hour's walk she reached the first customer, who stood in her doorway, dish in hand.

"I'll take ten tonight, my child," said the friendly woman.

She counted off ten and, with a greeting, continued on her way.

In three quarters of an hour the basket was empty, and Kathy stepped into the small general store. A pretty thimble and a bagful of sweets were soon put into the basket, and now Kathy turned back toward home. About halfway, she saw two of the girls who had teased her in the morning coming toward her. She bravely suppressed a longing to hide, and, her heart beating wildly, she went on.

"Look! Here comes Crazykate!"

At her wits' end, Kathy took the bag of sweets from her basket and politely held it out to the children. They quickly grabbed it from her and ran away with it. One of them stuck out her tongue at Kathy.

Lonesome and heartbroken, Kathy sat down in the grass at the edge of the road, and wept, wept, and wept. Finally, in the dark, she dried her tears, picked up the basket, and slowly set off in the direction of home.

Somewhere in the grass, the thimble glittered . . .

The Flower Girl

Every morning at seven-thirty the door of a little house at the edge of the village opens, and out steps a rather small girl, carrying a basket heaped with flowers on each arm. After shutting the door, she switches her burdens and starts the day's work. The people of the village, who answer her smiling nod as she passes, feel sorry for her. "That road is much too long and the job too hard," they think, "for a child of twelve."

But the little girl, herself, naturally doesn't know the thoughts of her fellow villagers. Merrily, and as quickly as her short legs will take her, she walks on and on and on. The road to the town is really very long; it takes her at least two and a half hours of steady walking to reach it and, with two heavy baskets, that's not easy.

When she finally trudges through the streets of the town she is exhausted, and it's only the prospect of soon being able to sit down and rest that sustains her. But the little one is brave and doesn't slow down her gait until she gets to her spot in the market. Then she sits down and waits and waits . . .

Sometimes she sits and waits all day because there are not enough people who want to buy something from the poor flower girl. Quite often Krista has to carry her baskets, still half full, back to the village in the evening.

But today things are different. It is Wednesday, and the market is unusually crowded and busy. Beside her, market women cry their wares, and all about her the little girl hears scolding and angry voices.

Passers-by can scarcely hear Krista, for her high little voice is almost drowned out in the market hubbub. But all day long, Krista doesn't stop calling, "Pretty flowers, a dime a bunch! Buy my pretty flowers!" Some people who, finished with their errands, take time to look into the baskets gladly pay a dime for one of the lovely small bouquets.

At twelve o'clock, Krista walks to the opposite side of the market square, where the owner of the coffee stand is in the habit of giving her, free of charge, a cupful with plenty of sugar. For this kind man Krista keeps her prettiest flowers.

Then she takes her seat again and once more starts crying her wares. At last, about three-thirty, she picks up her baskets and returns to the village. Now she walks much more slowly than she did in the morning. Krista is tired, terribly tired.

The trip back takes her a full three hours, and it is six-thirty when she reaches the door of the little old house. Inside everything is still the way she left it—cold, lonesome, and untidy. Her sister, with whom she shares the place, works in the village from early morning to late at night. Krista can't afford to rest; she is no sooner home than she begins to peel potatoes and clean vegetables. Her sister gets back from work at seven-thirty, and they finally sit down and have something to eat.

At eight in the evening the door of the cottage opens again, and once more the little girl comes out with the two big baskets on her arms. Now she walks into the fields that surround the little house. She doesn't have to go far; soon she bends down in the grass and picks flowers, all kinds of them, big ones and little ones, and all of them go into the baskets. The sun has almost set, and the child still sits in the grass, collecting her next day's supply.

The task is finished at last; the baskets are full. The sun has set, and Krista lies down in the grass, her hands folded under her head, and looks up into the sky.

This is her favorite quarter hour, and nobody need think that the hardworking little flower girl is dissatisfied. She never is and never will be so long as, every day, she may have this wonderful short rest.

In the field, amid the flowers, beneath the darkening sky, Krista is content. Gone is fatigue, gone is the market, gone are the people. The little girl dreams and thinks only of the bliss of having, each day, this short while alone with God and nature.

The Guardian Angel

February 22, 1944

Once upon a time, an old lady and her young granddaughter lived for many years on the very edge of a large forest. The girl's parents had died when she was still quite small, and the grandmother had always taken good care of her. The little house in which they lived was a lonesome place, but they didn't seem to realize it and were happy together.

One morning the old lady couldn't get up, because she was in great pain. Her granddaughter was now fourteen years old, and she looked after her grandma as well as she could. It lasted five days; then the grandmother died and the girl was all alone in that lonesome cottage. As she knew hardly anyone and did not want to call in strangers to bury her grandmother, she dug a grave under an old tree in the woods, and there laid her grandma to rest.

When the poor girl came back to the house, she felt utterly forsaken and very sad. She lay down on her bed and cried her heart out. She lay there all day and didn't get up until evening, to get a bite to eat. So it went, day after day. The poor child no longer took pleasure in anything and only mourned and mourned for her dear old granny.

Then something happened that changed her entirely in just one day. It was night, and the girl was asleep when, suddenly, her grandmother stood before her. She was dressed in white from head to foot; her white hair hung down her shoulders, and she carried a small lamp.

From her bed, the girl watched her and waited for the grandmother to speak. "My dear little girl," the grandma began, "I have been watching you now every day for four weeks, and you never do anything but weep and sleep. That is not good, and I have come to tell you that you must work and spin; that you must take care of our little house and also dress prettily again.

"You mustn't think that, now I am dead, I no longer look after you; I am in heaven and always watch you from above. I have become your guardian angel, and I am always with you, just as before. Take up your work again, darling, and never forget that your granny is with you!"

Then Granny disappeared, and the girl slept on.

Next morning when she awoke, she remembered what her grandmother had said, and she was filled with joy and no longer felt forsaken. She started working again, sold her spinning in the market, and followed her granny's advice at all times.

Later, much later, she also wasn't alone in the outside world. She was married to a fine man, a miller. She thanked her granny for not having left her alone, and she well knew that, though she now always had good company, her guardian angel would not leave her until the end of her days.

Fear

It was a terrible time through which I was living. The war raged about us, and nobody knew whether or not he would be alive the next hour. My parents, brothers, sisters, and I made our home in the city, but we expected that we either would be evacuated or have to escape in some other way. By day the sound of cannon and rifle shots was almost continuous, and the nights were mysteriously filled with sparks and sudden explosions that seemed to come from some unknown depth.

I cannot describe it; I don't remember that tumult quite clearly, but I do know that all day long I was in the grip of fear. My parents tried everything to calm me, but it didn't help. I felt nothing, nothing but fear; I could neither eat nor sleep—fear clawed at my mind and body and shook me. That lasted for about a week; then came an evening and a night which I recall as though it had been yesterday.

At half past eight, when the shooting had somewhat

died down, I lay in a sort of half doze on a sofa. Suddenly all of us were startled by two violent explosions. As though stuck with knives, we all jumped up and ran into the hall. Even Mother, usually so calm, looked pale. The explosions repeated themselves at pretty regular intervals. Then: a tremendous crash, the noise of much breaking glass, and an earsplitting chorus of yelling and screaming. I put on what heavy clothes I could find in a hurry, threw some things into a rucksack, and ran. I ran as fast as I could, ran on and on to get away from the fiercely burning mass about me. Everywhere shouting people darted to and fro; the street was alight with a fearsome red glow.

I didn't think of my parents or of my brothers and sisters. I had thoughts only for myself and knew that I must rush, rush, rush! I didn't feel any fatigue; my fear was too strong. I didn't know that I had lost my rucksack. All I felt and knew was that I had to run.

I couldn't possibly say how long I ran on with the image of the burning houses, the desperate people and their distorted faces before me. Then I sensed that it had got more quiet. I looked around and, as if waking up from a nightmare, I saw that there was nothing or no one behind me. No fire, no bombs, no people. I looked a little more closely and found that I stood in a meadow. Above me the stars glistened and the moon shone; it was brilliant weather, crisp but not cold.

I didn't hear a sound. Exhausted, I sat down on the grass, then spread the blanket I had been carrying on my arm, and stretched out on it.

I looked up into the sky and realized that I was no longer afraid; on the contrary, I felt very peaceful inside. The funny thing was that I didn't think of my family, nor yearn for them; I yearned only for rest, and it wasn't long before I fell asleep there in the grass, under the sky.

When I woke up the sun was just rising. I immediately knew where I was; in the daylight I recognized the houses at the outskirts of our city. I rubbed my eyes and had a good look around. There was no one to be seen; the dandelions and the clover-leaves in the grass were my only company. Lying back on the blanket for a while, I mused about what to do next. But my thoughts wandered off from the subject and returned to the wonderful feeling of the night before, when I sat in the grass and was no longer afraid.

Later I found my parents, and together we moved to another town. Now that the war is over, I know why my fear disappeared under the wide, wide heavens. When I was alone with nature, I realized—realized without actually knowing it—that fear is a sickness for which there is only one remedy. Anyone who is as afraid, as I was then, should look at nature and see that God is much closer than most people think.

Since that time I have never been afraid again, no matter how many bombs fell near me.

The Wise Old Dwarf

April 18, 1944

There once was a little elf called Dora. She was pretty and rich, and her parents spoiled her terribly. She was always laughing. She laughed from early morning until late at night; she was happy about everything and never gave sadness or sorrow a thought.

In the same forest where Dora made her home, there lived a dwarf by the name of Peldron. He was, in everything, the exact opposite of Dora. While Dora was forever smiling at all the beauty and goodness about her, Peldron worried because there was so much misery in the world, and especially in the world of elves and dwarves.

One day Dora had to do an errand at the shoemaker's in elves' village. And what do you think happened? She met that boring and long-faced Peldron. Dora was sweet but, because everyone liked her, she was a bit conceited, too. Boldly, she ran toward Peldron, grabbed his pretty dwarf's hat and, from a distance, laughed with the hat in her hands.

Peldron was really cross; he stamped on the ground and

called, "Give me back my hat, give it back immediately!"

But Dora did no such thing, ran farther away, and finally hid the hat in a hollow tree. Then she quickly continued on her way to the shoemaker.

After looking for it a long time, Peldron did find his hat. He couldn't take a joke, and especially not from Dora, whom he didn't like at all. Listlessly, he went on his way. Suddenly, a deep voice roused him from his brooding:

"Peldron, I am the oldest dwarf in the world, and also the poorest. Please, give me something, so that I may buy some food."

Peldron shook his head, no. "I won't give you anything," he said. "You had better die, so you needn't endure the misery of this world." And he hurried on without looking back.

Meanwhile, Dora, on her way back from the shoemaker, also met the old dwarf, and she, too, was asked for alms. Like Peldron, she refused, but for a different reason.

"I won't give you any money," she said. "If you are poor, it's your own fault. The world is so wonderful that I can't be bothered with poor people." And she skipped along.

With a sigh, the old dwarf sat down on a mossy spot, wondering what he should do with those two children. One was too sad, the other too gay, and both wouldn't get very far in life that way.

Now, this ancient dwarf was no ordinary, everyday dwarf; he was a sorcerer, but not an evil one. On the contrary, he wanted people and elves and dwarves to improve and the world to progress.

He sat there, thinking, for an hour. Then he rose and slowly walked to the house of Dora's parents.

The day after their meeting in the forest, Dora and Peldron found themselves locked up together in a small cabin. The old dwarf had taken them away to give them a proper training. The great sorcerer's wish was the same as a command, and even parents dared not disobey it.

What were those two to do in that hut? They weren't allowed to go out, nor were they permitted to quarrel. They had to work the whole day long! Those had been the old dwarf's orders. And so Dora worked, made jokes and laughed; and Peldron worked, looked gloomy and felt sad.

Every evening at seven, the old dwarf came to check on their work and then left again. They wondered how they could possibly get free. There was only one way, and that was to obey the old dwarf in everything.

You can't imagine how difficult it was for Dora to have to look at that long-jawed Peldron all day long; Peldron, Peldron, early and late, and never anybody else. But she hadn't much time to talk to him, anyway, even if she had wanted to, because she had to cook (she had learned that from her mother), keep the house clean and in order, and in her "spare time," if you please, get some spinning done.

Peldron, for his part, must chop wood in the enclosed garden, cultivate the grounds, and cobble shoes in the bargain. At seven in the evening, Dora called him to supper, and by that time they were both so tired that they could hardly talk to the old dwarf when he arrived on his nightly visit.

They kept this up for a week. Dora still laughed often, and yet she began to understand that there was a serious side to life. She realized that there were people who had a difficult time and that it was not asking too much to help such folk when they were in distress, instead of sending them away with some rude words. And Peldron lost a little of his gloom; it even happened, from time to time, that he whistled softly at his work, or grinned when he saw Dora laughing.

On Sunday they were both allowed to come with the old dwarf to chapel in elves' village. They paid more attention to the words of the dwarf-preacher than they had before, and they felt quite content as they walked back through the shady woods.

"Because you have been so good," said the old dwarf, "you may spend the day in the open, just as you used to do. But, mind you, tomorrow you go back to work. You can't go home, and you can't visit your friends."

Neither thought of running away; they were very glad to be permitted the freedom of the forest, even for one day. All that Sunday they played and had fun, watched the birds, the flowers and the blue sky, and enjoyed the warm sunshine. Happily, they returned to their cabin in the evening, slept until morning, and then went back to work.

The old dwarf made them lead this kind of life for four long months. Every Sunday morning they went to church, spent the rest of the day in the open, and worked hard the remainder of the week.

When the four months were up, the old dwarf one evening took both of them by the hand and walked into the woods with them.

"Look here, children," he said, "I am sure that you often have been angry with me. I also think that you both must be longing to go home."

"Yes," said Dora. And "Yes," echoed Peldron.

"But do you understand that this has been good for you?"

No, sir, they didn't understand that so well.

"Well, I will explain it," said the old dwarf. "I took you here and left you together to teach you that there are other things in this world beside YOUR fun and YOUR gloom. You both will get along in life much better than before you came here. Little Dora has become somewhat more serious, and Peldron has cheered up a bit, because you were obliged to make the best of having to live together. I also believe that you like each other better than before. Don't you agree, Peldron?"

"Yes," said Peldron, "I like Dora much better now."

"Well," said the old dwarf, "you may go back to your parents. But think often about your stay in the little cabin. Enjoy all the fine things life will bring you, but don't forget the sorrows of others and try to comfort them. All people, children, dwarves and elves can help one another.

"So, on your way, and don't be cross with me anymore. I have done for you what I could, and it was for your own good. Good day, children, till we meet again!"

"Bye-bye," said Dora and Peldron, and off they went to their homes.

Once more the old dwarf sat down in a shady spot. He had but one wish—that he might guide all the children of men into the right path, as he had guided those two.

And, truly, Dora and Peldron lived happily ever after! Once and for all they had learned the great lesson that people must laugh and weep, each at the right time. Later, much later, when they were grown up, they went to live together in a small house of their own free will, and Dora did the work inside and Peldron outside, just as they had when they were very young.

Blurry, the Explorer

April 23, 1944

Once, when he was still very small, Blurry felt a great desire to escape from the fussing care of his mother bear and see something of the wide, wide world for himself. For days he was much less playful than usual, so busy was he thinking over his plans. But on the evening of the fourth day, his mind was made up. His plan was ready and only awaited execution. Early in the morning he would go into the garden—very softly, of course, so that Mimi, his little mistress, wouldn't notice—then he would creep through a hole in the hedge, and after that, well, after that, he would discover the world! He did all this, and so quietly that nobody knew he had escaped before he had been gone several hours.

As he crept out from under the hedge, his fur was smeared with earth and mud, but a bear who wants to make a voyage of discovery mustn't mind a little thing like a few spots of dirt on his skin. So, looking straight ahead, so as not to stumble over the uneven cobblestones, Blurry stepped smartly in the direction of the street, which could be reached through the alley between the garden.

In the street he was a little frightened by the many grown-up people between whose legs he disappeared completely. "I must stay near the edge of the sidewalk," he told himself; "otherwise they'll run over me." And this was, indeed, the most sensible thing to do. Yes, Blurry was intelligent, which was self-evident because, tiny as he was, he wanted to see the world.

He kept close to the edge and saw to it that he wasn't caught between a pair of big, fast-moving feet. But suddenly his heart started pounding as if he had sledgehammers inside his chest . . . What was that? A big black abyss lay before his feet. It was an open cellar, but Blurry didn't know that, and he got dizzy. Must he go down in there? Terrified, he looked about, but the trousered men's legs and the skirted ladies' legs calmly walked around the gaping hole and acted as if nothing were amiss. Not quite recovered from the shock, step by little step, he followed their example, and it wasn't long before he could continue.

"Now I'm walking in the big world," thought Blurry, "but where IS the world? Because of all those trousers, skirts, and stockings, I cannot see the world at all. Perhaps I am too small to discover the world, but that doesn't matter. If I eat my porridge and swallow my cod-liver oil every day (he shuddered at the idea), I will get just as big as those people. Let's go on; sooner or later, in one way or another, I'll see the world."

He walked further and paid as little attention as possible to the many fat and thin, long and short legs around him. But must he just walk and walk and walk? He was getting hungry and it was also beginning to grow a bit dark.

Blurry had not given eating and sleeping any thought. He had been too much occupied with his plans of discovery to think of such ordinary and unheroic things as eating and sleeping.

Sighing, he walked on for a while until he discovered an open door. He hesitated on the threshold and then quietly went in. He was in luck, for, after passing through another door, he saw two saucers standing on the floor between some wooden legs. One of the saucers was filled with milk; the other with some sort of food. Starving, Blurry drank every drop of the milk. Then he ate the delicious food in the other saucer and felt entirely satisfied.

But, oh, what was THAT? Something white with green eyes approached slowly, staring at him. Directly in front of him, it stopped and asked in a strange small voice:

"Who are you, and why have you eaten all my food?"

"I am Blurry, and, on a voyage of discovery, a fellow needs something to eat. But I really didn't know that it belonged to you."

"So, you are on a voyage of discovery. But how is it that you had to discover just MY saucer?"

"Because I didn't see any other," Blurry answered in an unfriendly tone. Then he thought better of it, and asked in a kindlier manner:

"But what is your name, and what kind of strange creature are you?"

"I am Muriel and I belong to the family of Angora cats. I am very valuable, at least my mistress always says so. But you know, Blurry, I am forever alone and am often bored. Won't you stay with me for a while?"

"I will stay and sleep here," said Blurry, as though he were doing Muriel a favor. "But tomorrow, I must go on and discover the world."

As a beginning, this seemed fair enough to Muriel.

"Come along," she said, and Blurry followed her to another room where he again saw nothing but wooden legs. Still there was something else. In a corner stood a big wicker basket in which lay a pillow covered with green silk. Muriel stepped onto the pillow with her dirty feet, but Blurry thought it a pity to soil things that way. "Shan't I first wash up a bit?" he asked. "I'll wash you, just as I wash myself," replied Muriel. Blurry was not acquainted with that method, and that was a good thing, for had he known he wouldn't have permitted Muriel to start.

Now the cat told him to stand up straight and calmly ran her tongue over his feet. It made Blurry shiver and he asked if that was her usual way of taking and giving baths.

"Yes, it is," she said. "You will see how clean you'll get; you will shine, and a shiny bear has entree everywhere and so finds it much easier to discover the world." Blurry controlled his shivers and uttered no complaint, brave bear. Muriel's bath seemed to take hours; Blurry was getting a little impatient, and his feet hurt from standing so long, but finally he did shine. Muriel again stepped into the basket and Blurry, who was exhausted, lay down. In less than five minutes they were both asleep.

Next morning Blurry awoke, and it took him a while to realize where he was. Muriel snored a little, and Blurry badly wanted his breakfast. Without considering the comfort of his hostess, he shook her and started to give her orders:

"Give me my breakfast, please, Muriel; I am awfully hungry."

The pretty Angora puss first had a good yawn, stretched to twice her usual length, and answered:

"No, no, you get nothing more. My lady mustn't notice that you are here; you must leave, as quickly as possible, through the garden."

Muriel jumped out of the basket, took Blurry along through the room, out of the door, into another door, and then again out of a door, this time a glass one, and they were outside. "Bon voyage, Blurry," she said. "Till we meet again!" And she was gone.

Lonesome and no longer convinced of his cleverness, Blurry walked through the garden and then, through the hole in the hedge, into the street. Where should he go, and how long would it take to discover the world? Blurry didn't know. Very slowly he walked along when, suddenly, a big four-legged thing ran toward him at full speed. It made tremendous noises so that Blurry, almost deafened and shaking with fear, clung to the side of a house. The gigantic thing halted, and Blurry began to cry from fear. The monster, not a bit disturbed by this, sat down and did nothing but stare at the poor little bear with his big eyes. Blurry pulled himself together. "What do you want of me?" he asked.

"I only want to take a look at you, because I've never seen anything like you."

Blurry breathed a sigh of relief. After all, one could talk, even with this ogre. Here was a curious thing, Blurry thought; why couldn't his own little mistress ever understand him? But he didn't have much time to consider this weighty question, for the big beast opened his mouth wide, showing all his huge cruel teeth. This made Blurry shiver worse than he had during Muriel's washing session. What would the monster do to him? He soon found out, for the beast, without a by-your-leave or with-your-leave, grabbed him by the neck and dragged him through the street.

Blurry couldn't cry, for he would have choked to death

if he had; shouting was also out of the question. All that was left him was to shudder, and that didn't give a fellow any courage. He didn't have to walk now; if his neck hadn't hurt so, it wouldn't have been too bad; it was like a ride.

After all, it could be worse. But you did get woozy in the head from that continuous pushing. Where, where, is he taking me? Where? . . . Blurry, held fast by the animal, had dozed off. But the nap didn't last long. The beast suddenly was at a loss to know why he carried this thing in his teeth. Carelessly, he dropped him and ran off. And there lay the helpless little bear who wanted to discover the world, all alone with his pain. Bravely, he rose in order not to be trampled upon, rubbed his eyes, and looked around.

Far fewer legs, far fewer people, much more sun, and fewer cobbles under his feet. Could this be the world? There was no room in his poor head for thoughts; everything hurt and hammered in there. He didn't want to walk anymore. Why should he? Muriel was far away, his mother still farther, and his little mistress . . . No! He was on his way, and he must persist until he had discovered the world.

A sound behind him startled him, and he turned around, hoping that no other beast was going to bite him. No, it was a little girl.

"Look, Mama, a little bear! May I take him along?"

"No, my dear, he is sick. Look, he is bleeding."

"That doesn't matter, Mama; we can wash it off when we get home. Then I'll have something to play with."

Blurry didn't understand a word of this conversation; little bears know only animal talk. But the little blond girl looked so sweet that he didn't resist when he was wrapped in a scarf and put into a bag.

So, swaying to and fro, Blurry continued his voyage through the world. After they had walked for a time, Blurry, with the scarf still around him, was taken out of the bag, and the girl carried him on her arm. That was a piece of luck, for now he could see the road from above. What big piles of stones, very high, with here and there a white opening! And, way on top, almost to the' sky, there was a swirl of smoke. That must be for decoration, just like the feather on his little mistress' hat. Wasn't that funny?

Below, on the road, something said "toot-toot" and ran very fast, though it had no legs, only some round, blown-up things. Say what you like, it was worth the trouble to go discover the world! What was the use of always staying home? Why were you born? Surely not to stick forever with your mother. No, see and experience things, that was the way to grow up! Yes, Blurry knew what he wanted.

At long last the girl stopped at a door. She went in, and the first thing Blurry saw was something on the order of Muriel. This one was called Puss, if Blurry remembered right. This Puss stroked the legs of the blond girl, but she pushed him away and took Blurry to a white thing. It was high above the ground, wide and smooth. At the side, there was something of shiny metal which could be turned. This the blond girl did, and she set him down on a hard, cold place. Then the girl began to wash him, especially that part of his fur where that nasty beast had bitten him. It hurt a lot and Blurry cried, but no one seemed to mind.

Fortunately, this wash didn't last as long as the one Muriel had given him, but it was colder and much wetter. The girl finished her task pretty quickly, dried him, wrapped him in a fresh scarf, and put him in a down bed, just like the one his little mistress had for him. But why go to bed? Blurry wasn't the least bit tired and didn't want to go to sleep. The girl was no sooner out of the room than he slid out of bed and, by way of a large number of doors and holes, landed once more in the street.

"I must get something to eat," thought Blurry. He sniffed; "Yes, there ought to be something good around here, for you can smell it."

He followed his nose and soon stood at the door from which the fine aroma came. He slipped into the big store between the stockinged legs of a lady. Behind a big high something stood two girls. They quickly caught sight of him. They must have worked hard all day long and could use a little help, for they picked him up at once and placed him in a rather dark space where it was very, very hot.

That wasn't so bad; the main thing was that you could eat there as much as you pleased. On the floor and on low shelves, there lay rows of buns, rolls, and pastries, prettier than any Blurry had ever seen. What, after all, HAD Blurry seen? Not so much, come to think of it. Hungrily, he attacked the good things and ate so much that he almost got sick.

Then he took another thorough look around. There was really much to be seen here, it looked like a sweet-tooth's paradise. Everywhere loaves of bread, rolls, tarts, cookies, just for the taking!

And it was very busy here. Blurry saw many white legs, very different from those in the street. But there wasn't much time for dreaming; the girls, who had been standing at a little distance, pushed a broom into his hands and showed him how to use it. Sweep the floor—

Blurry knew all about it—he had seen his mother do it. But it wasn't as easy as it looked. He tried bravely, but the broom was big and heavy, and the dust tickled his nose so that he had to sneeze.

And it was so hot; he felt more and more uncomfortable from the work he wasn't used to and the heat, but each time he stopped to rest for a minute, somebody put him back to work and gave him a slap besides.

"If only I hadn't walked in here so hastily," he thought, "then I would have been spared all this heavy work." But there was nothing he could do about it. He had to sweep, and sweep he did. When he had swept a long time, so long that the dirt lay in a big heap in a corner, one of the girls took him by the hand and led him to a spot where some hard yellow shavings lay on the floor. They told him to lie down, and Blurry understood that he was allowed to sleep.

He stretched out as if the shavings were a comfortable bed, and he slept until the next morning. At seven o'clock he had to get up, was again permitted to eat all he wanted, and once more was put to work. Poor Blurry, he wasn't even rested. He wasn't used to working and the heat bothered him terribly. His little head, arms, and legs ached, and he felt as if every part of him was swollen.

Now for the first time, he began to long for home, for his mother, his little mistress, his soft bed, and the nice lazy life; but how would he ever get there? Escape was out of the question; they kept a sharp eye on him and, besides, the only door to the street was in the room where the two girls worked all day long. No, Blurry simply had to bide his time. His thoughts were confused, he felt dizzy and weak. Everything about him started to turn; he sat down—nobody told him not to. When he felt a little better, he went back to work.

After a week of sweeping from morning until evening, he scarcely knew anything else. Little bears forget quickly, and that is a good thing. But he had not forgotten his mother and his home; only they seemed so unreal and so very far away!

One evening the two girls who had caught Blurry read this advertisement in the newspaper:

REWARD FOR THE RETURN OF A SMALL BROWN BEAR
WHO ANSWERS TO THE NAME OF BLURRY.

"Do you think that could be our little bear?" they asked each other. "He doesn't work very hard; in fact, you can't expect it from such a small creature. If we get a reward for returning him, we will be better off than we are now."

They ran to the back of the store and yelled, "Blurry!"

Blurry looked up from his work; had anyone called him? The big broom fell from his hands; how did they know his name? The girls came closer, and once more they called, "Blurry!"

He ran toward them. "Yes, his name is Blurry, all right," one of the girls said to the other. "Let us take him back tonight." Agreed. That same evening, Blurry was delivered to the home of his little mistress, and the girls got their reward.

Blurry's little mistress gave him a spanking for his disobedience, and then a kiss because he was safely home again. His mother only asked:

"Blurry, why did you run away?"

"I wanted to discover the world," was his answer.

"And did you discover it?"

"Oh, I have seen very, very much. I have become a very experienced bear."

"Yes, I know all that; but I asked you if you had discovered the world."

"No, no . . . not really; you see, I couldn't find it!"

The Fairy

May 12, 1944

That fairy I am talking about was no ordinary fairy of whom you find so many in fairyland. Oh, no, my fairy was a very special fairy, special in her appearance and special in her way of doing things. Why, everybody is sure to ask, was that fairy so special?

Well, because she didn't just help somebody here, and make some fun there, but because she had set herself the task of bringing happiness to the world and to all people.

This special fairy was called Ellen. Her parents had died when she was still quite little and had left her money. So Ellen could do as she chose and buy everything she wanted, even as a small girl. Other children, fairies and elves would get spoiled in that way, but not Ellen. As she grew older, she spent her money only to buy pretty clothes and delicious things to eat.

One morning Ellen lay awake in her soft bed, wondering what to do with all her money. "I can't use it all myself," she thought, "and I can't take it with me into the grave. Why shouldn't I use it to make others happy?"

That was a good plan, and Ellen wanted to carry it out at once. She rose, dressed, took a small wicker basket, put into it part of one of her bundles of money, and went out.

"Where shall I begin?" she asked herself. "I know. The widow of the wood chopper is sure to be pleased with a visit of mine. Her husband has just died, and the poor lady must be having a difficult time."

Singing, Ellen walked through the grass and knocked at the door of the wood chopper's cottage. "Enter!" came a voice from the inside. Ellen softly opened the door and looked into a darkened room. In a far corner a little old woman sat knitting in a shabby armchair.

She was surprised as Ellen entered and immediately laid a handful of money on the table. Like everybody else, the woman knew that one must not refuse the gifts of fairies and elves.

"That is very sweet of you, little one," she said. "There are not many people who make gifts without expecting something in return, but happily the folk of fairyland are an exception."

Ellen looked at her in amazement. "What did you mean by that?" she asked.

"I simply meant that there are few who give and not want something back."

"Is that so? But why should I want something from you? I am glad that my basket is a little lighter."

"Good!" said the old lady. "Thank you very much."

Ellen bade her good-bye and left. In ten minutes, she had reached the next cottage. Here she also knocked, though she didn't know the people. She hadn't been there long before she understood that money was not a problem here. The people did not lack *things*—they were poor in happiness. The lady of the house received her kindly, but she seemed to have no sparkle; her eyes were dull and she looked sad. Ellen decided to remain here a little longer.

"Perhaps I can help this lady in some other way," she thought, and really, when the sweet little fairy had seated herself upon a cushion, the woman began to talk about her troubles without being asked.

She spoke of her wicked husband, of her naughty children, and all her other misfortunes. Ellen listened, put in a question now and then, and became much concerned about the woman's sorrow.

When the woman had finished her story, Ellen spoke.

"Dear lady," she said, "I don't know about such things from experience, and I know even less how to help you. But, just the same, I'd like to give you some advice, which I, myself, always follow when I feel lonesome and sad.

"One fine morning, take a walk through the big forest until you reach the moor. Then, after walking a while in the heather, sit down somewhere and do nothing. Only look at the blue sky and the trees, and you will gradually feel peaceful inside and realize that nothing is so hopelessly bad that something can't be done to improve it— even a little."

"No," said the lady. "That remedy will help just as much as all the other pills I have swallowed."

"Try it, anyway," urged the fairy. "Alone with nature, all worries leave one. You grow first quiet, and then glad, and feel that God has not deserted you."

"If it will please you," said the woman, "I will try it one day."

"Fine. If I may, I will drop in again next week at this time."

And so Ellen went from house to house, cheering and

comforting people, and at the end of the long day her basket was empty and her heart full; she knew that she had put her money to better use than by buying clothes. From that day on, Ellen often went on her rounds. She wore her yellow flowered frock, her hair was tied with a big bow, and she carried her basket on her arm. That's how she looked when she made her visits.

Even the woman who had enough money but too much trouble was beginning to feel happier. Ellen knew it; her remedy always worked.

The fairy gained many friends—not other fairies and elves, but people and children. The children told her everything, and this gave her much insight and the ability to have the right word of comfort on every occasion.

But so far as her money was concerned, she had miscalculated. After about a year, she had just enough left to live on.

Now, whoever thinks that this made Ellen sad and kept her from offering gifts is mistaken. She continued to give much, not money, but good advice and loving, healing words. She had learned that, even if one is all alone, he can still make his life beautiful; and no matter how poor one is, he can still give others riches.

When Ellen died, a very old fairy, there was more mourning in the land than there had ever been before. But Ellen's spirit was not gone. When people slept, she returned to give them blissful dreams; even in their slumber they received the gift of wise counsel from this very special fairy.

Rita

It was a quarter past four, and I was walking through a rather quiet street. I had just decided to drop in at the nearest pastry shop when, from a sidestreet, there came a couple of teen-aged girls who, chatting busily, walked arm-in-arm in the direction I had chosen.

From time to time it is interesting and refreshing to listen to the conversation of teen-aged girls, not only because they laugh at the merest trifle, but also because their laughter is so infectious that everyone in their vicinity must involuntarily laugh with them.

So I walked stealthily behind the pair and eavesdropped on their talk, which had to do with the buying of sweets for ten cents. They consulted each other seriously on what to get for their money, and one could tell that their mouths watered at the thought of it. At the pastry shop, they continued their chat while looking at the wares in the show window.

As I, too, was fairly eating the delicious things with my eyes, I knew what their choice would be before they stepped into the shop. Inside it wasn't busy, and the girls were served at once. They had picked two fruit tarts which, wonder above wonder, they managed to take, untouched, out of the store.

A minute later I also was ready, and once more the two walked, talking loudly, ahead of me. On the next corner there was another pastry shop, in front of whose window there stood little girl, taking in the display with greedy eyes. Soon the three were talking together, and I reached the corner in time to hear one of the teen-agers ask:

"Are you hungry, little one? Would you like a fruit tart?"

The tiny one, of course, said, "Yes."

"Don't be foolish, Rita," said the other teen-ager. "Put your tart quickly into your mouth, as I did, for if you give it to this kid, you'll have nothing."

Rita didn't answer but stood there undecided for a moment, looking from the tart to the little girl and back again. Then she suddenly gave the child the pastry and said:

"Please, eat this, my dear; I'm going home to dinner, anyway."

And before the little one could thank her, Rita and her friend had disappeared. As I passed the youngster, who had taken a big bite from the tart with obvious relish, she offered it to me.

"Have a taste, miss; I got this for a present."

I thanked her and, smiling, I walked on. Who do you think got the most pleasure from the fruit tart—Rita, her friend, or the little girl?

I think it was Rita.

Jackie

Jackie stands at the open window in her little room and breathes the fresh air. She's hot and the bit of fresh air feels good on her tearstained face.

She raises her eyes higher and higher, until at last she's looking up at the stars and the moon.

"Oh," Jackie thinks. "I can't go on. I haven't even the strength to be sad. Paul has left me, I'm all alone, maybe for good, I just can't go on, I can't do anything, all I know is that I'm in despair." And while Jackie looks, looks at the things of nature, which show her all their beauty that day, she grows calm. As gust after gust of wind blows through the trees outside the house, as the sky darkens and the stars hide behind big, thick clouds, which look like bundles of blotting paper in the cloudy light and take on every conceivable shape, Jackie suddenly feels that her despair is gone, that she's still capable of doing something, and that no one can take away the happiness she feels inside her. "No one can do that," she whispers without knowing it. "Not even Paul."

After standing at the window for an hour, Jackie has recovered; she is still sad, but no longer in despair. Anyone who looks at nature, which is the same as looking into oneself, long and deeply enough, will, like Jackie, be cured of all despair.

Cady's Life

When Cady opened her eyes, the first thing she saw was that everything was white all around her. The last thing she remembered clearly was someone shouting at her . . . a car . . . then she fell down, and then everything was dark. She felt a sharp pain in her right leg and left arm, and without knowing it she sighed softly. Just after that a friendly face bent over her, looking out from under a white cap.

"Are you in great pain, poor thing? Do you remember what happened to you?" the nurse asked.

"It's nothing . . ."

The nurse smiled. Cady went on, speaking with difficulty: "Yes . . . a car, I fell . . . then nothing."

"Never mind. Just tell me your name. Then your parents will be able to come and see you and they won't have to worry anymore."

Cady was visibly horrified. "But . . . but, but . . ." that was all she could say.

"Don't worry, your parents haven't been waiting for you so very long. You've only been here with us for an hour or so."

Cady managed a bit of a smile.

"My name is Caroline Dorothea Van Altenhoven, Cady for short. My address is 261 Zuider Amstellaan."

"Do you miss your parents very much?"

Cady only nodded. She was so tired, and everything hurt so badly; just one more sigh and she had fallen asleep.

Sister Ank, who kept watch beside the bed in the little white room, looked anxiously at the little pale face that lay on the pillow as peacefully as if nothing were wrong. But something was very wrong. The child had been hit by a car that had come around the corner just as she was crossing the street. As the doctor had thought, she had a compound fracture, her left arm was crushed and something was wrong with her left foot, too.

There was a soft knock at the door; a nurse admitted a lady of medium height, followed by an unusually tall, handsome man. Sister Ank stood up; it was bound to be Cady's parents. Mrs. Van Altenhoven was very pale and looked at her daughter out of frightened eyes. Cady didn't notice, for she was still sleeping peacefully.

"Oh, Sister, tell me what happened to her. We waited and waited, but we never thought of an accident, oh, no . . ."

"You mustn't worry too much, Mrs. Van Altenhoven. Your daughter has already regained consciousness." Sister Ank told them as much about the case as she herself knew. She made it sound much less serious than it was, and that made her too feel a lot more cheerful. Maybe the child would recover after all.

While the grown-ups stood talking, Cady woke up, and
when she saw her parents in the room, she suddenly felt
much sicker than when she had been alone with the nurse.
She was assailed by thoughts; horrible visions came at her
from all sides, she saw herself crippled for life . . . with
only one arm, and all sorts of terrifying visions.

Then Mrs. Van Altenhoven noticed that Cady was
awake and went over to the bed.

"Are you in great pain? How are you now? Would you
like me to stay with you? Is there anything you need?"

Cady couldn't possibly answer all those questions. She
only nodded and longed for the moment when all the commotion would be over.

"Father!" That was all she could say.

Mr. Van Altenhoven sat down on the edge of the big
iron bed and, without saying a word or asking any questions, took his daughter's hand in his.

"Thank you, oh, thank you . . ." Cady said no more,
she had fallen asleep.

CHAPTER 2

A week had passed since the accident. Cady's mother
came to see her every morning and afternoon, but they
didn't let her stay very long, because she wore Cady out
with her incessant nervous chatter, and it was plain to the
nurse who always took care of Cady that she was much
more eager to see her father than her mother.

The nurse had very little trouble with the patient who
had been entrusted to her care; though Cady must often
have been in great pain, especially when the doctor was
examining her, she never complained and was never dissatisfied.

What she liked best was to lie still and daydream. Sister Ank sat beside her bed with a book or her knitting. After the first few days Cady didn't sleep so much. Then she was glad to chat awhile and there was no one she'd rather have chatted with than Sister Ank, who was calm and always spoke gently; it was her gentleness that Cady liked best. As she now began to realize, it was this motherly tenderness that she had always felt the lack of. Little by little, a feeling of confidence grew up between the nurse and Cady.

One morning, when the first two weeks had passed and Cady had told her a good deal, Sister Ank tactfully asked about Cady's mother. Cady had expected the question, and she was glad to be able to tell someone how she felt.

"What makes you ask me that? Has it struck you that I'm not nice to my mother?"

"No, not exactly. But I have a feeling that you're not so fond of your mother as of your father."

"You're right. I can't feel any real affection for my mother, and I have been very unhappy about it. Mother is so very different from me; in itself that wouldn't matter, but she has no understanding for things that I think important and that mean a lot to me. Can you help me, Sister Ank? Can you tell me how to be nicer to my mother, so she won't feel that I don't care for her as much as for Father? I know Mother loves me very much, I'm her only child."

"Yes, your mother means well, I think she just can't strike the right note. Maybe she's just a little bashful in her own way."

"Oh no. She's not bashful. Mother thinks her behavior is just right for a mother, she'd be speechless with amazement if anyone told her there was anything wrong with the tone she takes with me. Mother doesn't doubt for a moment that I'm entirely to blame. Sister Ank, you're just the mother I'd like to have. I so long for a real mother, and the woman who is my mother will never fill that place. I'm sure no one in all the world has everything they could ask for, though most people think I want for nothing. I have a cheerful home, Father and Mother get along well, they give me everything I could possibly want, and yet, isn't a real, understanding mother an important thing in a girl's life? And maybe not just a girl's. How do I know what boys think and feel? I've never known a boy at all well. I'm sure they have exactly the same need for an understanding mother, but maybe in a different way. Now it suddenly comes to me what's wrong with Mother, she has no tact. She has such a horrid way of talking about the most delicate things, she has no idea what's going on inside me, and yet she keeps saying how interested she is in young people. She has no idea what patience and gentleness are; she's a woman, but she's not a real mother."

"Don't be so hard on your mother, Cady. If she is different, maybe it's because she has suffered a good deal. Maybe that's why she doesn't like to talk about the delicate things."

"I don't know. What does a daughter like me know about the life of her parents? About her mother's life? Does anyone tell her? Mother doesn't understand me and I don't understand her. That's why there has never been any trust between us."

"And your father, Cady?"

"Father knows Mother and I don't get along. He understands Mother and he understands me. He's a darling, Sister Ank, he tries to make up to me for what Mother doesn't give me. Only he's afraid to talk about it, he never talks to me about anything that might involve Mother. A man can do a lot, but he can never take the place of a mother."

"I'd like to contradict you, Cady, but I can't, because I know you're right. I think it's a great shame that your mother and you are far apart instead of being close friends. Do you suppose things will never get better, not even when you're older?"

Almost imperceptibly Cady shrugged her shoulders. "Sister Ank, I miss a mother terribly. I'd be so glad to have someone I could trust completely and who would trust me too."

Cady fell silent and Sister Ank looked very grave. "Let's not talk about it anymore, child, but I'm glad you've told me all this about your mother."

CHAPTER 3

The weeks passed rather monotonously for Cady. A good many friends and acquaintances came to see her, but most of the time she was alone. Now she was well enough to sit up and read. She was given a bed table and her father brought her a diary; now she often sat writing her thoughts and feelings. Cady had never known that writing could give her so much pleasure.

Life in the hospital was very monotonous. Every day the same schedule, everything by the clock, never a mistake. Besides, it was so quiet, and Cady, who had no more pain in her arm and leg, would have liked a little more life and commotion around her. But, in spite of it all, the time passed rather quickly. Cady was never bored, and people gave her games that she could play all by her-

self with her right hand. And she didn't neglect her school
books, but devoted a certain amount of time each day to
them. She had been lying there for three months, but it
would soon be over. Her fractures were not as serious as
had been thought at first, and now that she was on the
mend the doctors thought it advisable that she should go
to a sanatorium to be fully cured.

So the following week Mrs. Van Altenhoven packed
Cady's things and she and her mother rode in an ambu-
lance for hours and finally reached the sanatorium. There
her days were even lonelier. Visitors came once or twice a
week, there was no Sister Ank, and everything was unfamiliar. Her only ray of light was that her health was
improving.

When she was settled in at the sanatorium and the cast
was removed from her arm, she had to learn to walk
again. That was terrible! Leaning on two nurses, she
moved one foot and then the other, and every day the
exercise began again. But the more she walked the better
it went and her legs soon got used to the movement.

It was a feast when she was well enough and had made
sufficient progress in her walking to go out into the garden
with a nurse and a cane. When the weather was fine,
Cady and Sister Truus, who always went with her,
would sit down on a bench in the big garden and talk or
read something, if they had taken a book with them. One
day they went into the woods outside the garden, and
since Cady liked that much better, the nurse raised no
objection. Of course Cady had to walk very slowly, and
often an unexpected movement gave her pain, but every
day she looked forward to this half hour out in the open,
where she could imagine that she was well again.

CHAPTER 4

Three weeks later, when she knew the path and every side path by heart, the doctor asked if she thought it would be more fun to go walking by herself. Cady thought it would be wonderful: "Can I really do that?"

"Yes, indeed. Go right out, and don't let us see you again," the doctor joked.

So when Cady was ready, she took her cane and went out by herself. It was a strange feeling, she was so used to having Sister Truus with her, but that first day she wasn't allowed beyond the garden gate. When the half hour was over, the duty nurse saw her coming in with redder cheeks than usual and a cheerful face.

"I see you've enjoyed your walk."

From that day on she could be seen every day in the garden, and soon it went so well that they gave her permission to go a little way outside the gate. The country around the sanatorium was very quiet, there were hardly any houses nearby, except for the big villas that were ten minutes' walk from there and also ten minutes' walk from one another.

On one of the side paths Cady discovered a bench consisting of a felled tree trunk. She took blankets out with her to make herself comfortable. Every morning she went there and sat daydreaming or reading. When she took a book along, it often fell from her hands after she had read a few pages, and she thought to herself: Isn't it a lot nicer just to sit here and look around; isn't it a lot better to think about the world and what's in it than to read what happens to this girl in the book? And then she looked around her, looked at the birds and the flowers, watched an ant at her feet, who was racing along with a tiny little twig, and she was happy. Then she dreamed of the time when she'd be able to run and jump again and go wherever she pleased, and she came to the conclusion that her accident, which had brought her so much misery, also had its good sides. She suddenly realized that here in the woods, in the sanatorium and in the silent hours spent in the hospital, she had found out something new about herself, discovered that she was a human being with feelings, thoughts and opinions of her own, a being separate from all others, a person in her own right.

Why had she never thought of that before, why had it never occurred to her to think about the people around her, or even about her own parents?

What was it Sister Ank had said? "Maybe it's because she has suffered so much that she doesn't like to talk about the delicate things in life?" And what had she herself answered? "What does a daughter know about her parents' life?"

How had she hit on that rather embittered answer, when she was positive that she had never before given the question a thought? And yet, wouldn't she have given the same answer at present? Wasn't her answer the truth? What does a child know about the lives of other people, her friends, her family, her teachers; what does she know about them except the externals? Had she ever spoken seriously with one of them? Deep in her heart she felt ashamed of this, though she had no idea how to go about learning something about people, and so she concluded: What good does it do me to have their confidence if I can't help them in their difficulties? And though she knew she didn't know how to help, she also knew how comforting it is to take someone into your confidence; not so long ago, she herself had been so unhappy about not having someone she could really talk to. Wasn't the crushing loneliness she herself sometimes felt just that? Wouldn't her loneliness go away if she had a friend whom she could tell everything? And Cady knew very well that she hadn't done enough, but also that others had never troubled their heads over her.

CHAPTER 5

Cady was cheerful by nature, she liked to chat. But if she was lonely, it wasn't for lack of opportunity to chat. No, that wasn't it; her sense of being alone was something else.

Hey there, Cady said to herself, now you're thinking again. Better watch your step, you'll go crazy if you keep circling around the same point. Cady gave herself a mental slap and couldn't help laughing a little at the crazy thought that there was no one around to scold her, and she probably missed it, and that was why she was always scolding herself.

Suddenly she looked up, she heard footsteps approaching and she'd never seen anyone on this out-of-the-way path. The steps came closer and closer and then out of the woods stepped a young man of about seventeen, who gave her a friendly good day and walked on.

"Who can that be?" she thought. "Could it be one of the villa people? Yes, that must be it, because nobody else lives around here." That disposed of the matter for Cady and she forgot all about the young man until he came by again the next morning and then for weeks after that, every morning at the same time.

One morning, when Cady was sitting on her bench and the boy came out of the woods, he stopped, held out his hand and said: "I'm Hans Donkert; we've known each other a long time now, why shouldn't we really get acquainted?"

"My name is Cady Van Altenhoven," said Cady. "And I think it's nice of you to stop for a change."

"Well, you see, I didn't know if you'd think it was silly of me to keep going by without stopping or if it would be all right to speak to you, but in the end I was so curious that I took the chance."

"Do I look as if someone should be afraid to speak to me?" Cady asked in a mischievous tone.

"Now that I see you close up," said Hans, taking up her joke, "you don't. But tell me this. The fact is I just wanted to ask you if you live in one of the villas or if you're a patient at the sanatorium—which seems most unlikely," he added quickly.

"Unlikely?" Cady couldn't help asking. "Why, of course I'm at the sanatorium. I broke my arm and my leg and crushed my foot, and it's taken me six months to get well."

"All that at once?"

"Yes, I was stupid enough to get myself run over. But don't get upset, it can't be as bad as all that if you yourself didn't take me for a patient." Hans was indeed rather upset, but he thought it best to say no more on the subject. "I live at Dennegroen House, back there." He pointed with his index finger. "You probably wonder why I pass here so regularly; I'm on vacation, I'm home from school, but every morning I go and see a friend of mine, because otherwise I get bored."

Cady made a move to stand up and Hans, who saw what she was about, held out his hand, because it was still hard for her. But Cady was stubborn, she declined his help. "Don't be offended, but I must try to get up by myself." Hans, who wanted to be helpful, took her book, and that gave him an excuse to escort the nice girl to the sanatorium. At the gate they said good-bye as though they'd known each other for ages, and Cady wasn't the least bit surprised when Hans arrived a little earlier than usual the next morning and sat down beside her on the tree trunk.

They spoke of many things but they never went very deep and Cady, who thought Hans was terribly nice, soon began to feel sorry that their conversation never touched on anything but the most everyday subjects. One morning they were sitting on the tree trunk not far from each other. For once the conversation just didn't flow. In the end, it dried up completely and they sat staring into space. Suddenly Cady, who had been deep in thought, looked up. She had a feeling that someone was looking at her. And true enough, Hans had been looking into the little face beside him for some time. And then their eyes met, they looked at each other longer than they actually wanted to, until Cady finally noticed what was happening and quickly lowered her eyes.

"Cady," said his voice beside her. "Cady, couldn't you tell me something about what's going on inside you?"

Cady thought it over for a moment; then she answered: "It's so hard, you won't understand. You're sure to think it's childish." Cady's courage had suddenly failed her, and on the last words her voice faltered.

"Have you so little confidence in me? Do you think I have no thoughts and feelings that I wouldn't confide in just anybody?"

"Of course I have confidence in you, that's not what I meant. But it's so hard. I myself don't know what I want to tell you." They both looked at the ground and their faces were grave. Cady noticed that Hans was terribly dis-

appointed, and since she felt sorry, she said suddenly:
"Do you too sometimes feel so alone, even when you have
friends near you? So alone inside, I mean."

"I believe that everyone who is young feels alone at
times, some more, some less. I do too, and up until now
I've never been able to talk to anyone about it. Boys don't
confide in their friends as easily as girls do. They're
much more afraid of not being understood and of being
laughed at."

He fell silent and Cady looked at him for a moment.
Then she said: "I've often wondered why people have so
little confidence in one another, why they're so reluctant
to pour out their hearts. Sometimes a. few words can clear
up terrible difficulties and misunderstandings."

Again neither of them spoke for some time. Then Cady
suddenly seemed to take a decision. "Hans," she asked,
"do you believe in God?"

"Yes, I believe in Him with all my heart."

"I've thought about God a good deal lately, but never
talked about Him. At home I learned when I was very
little to pray to God every night before I went to bed. It
was a habit, just like brushing my teeth. I didn't really
stay with God, I don't think He was in my thoughts at
all, because *people* could give me all I needed at that time.
Now that I've had this accident and I'm alone so much, I
have plenty of time to think about these things. On one of
my first evenings here, I got stuck in my prayer, and then
I noticed that I was thinking about something entirely different. So I made a change, I began to think about the
deeper meaning of the words, and then I made a discovery that there's a frightful lot more than I'd ever imagined
in this seemingly simple child's prayer. From then on I
prayed for different things, things I myself thought beau-

tiful, and not just a general prayer. But one evening a few weeks later I got stuck in my prayer again, and like lightning the thought flashed through my mind: 'Seeing that I never gave God a thought when I had it good, why should He help me now in my hour of need?' That question has stayed with me, because I know it would be only right and just for God not to think of me now."

"I can't quite agree with you on that last point. In the past, when you were leading a happy life, you prayed mechanically, your prayers had no content, you hardly gave God a thought. But now that you're looking for Him because you're in pain and fear, now that you're really trying to be as you think you should, I'm sure God won't leave you in the lurch. Trust Him, Cady, He has helped so many people."

Thoughtfully, Cady looked up at the trees. "But, Hans, how do we know that God exists? Who and what is God; no one has ever seen Him, after all; sometimes I have the feeling that praying to Him is praying to the air."

"When you ask me who and what God is, I can only say: No one can tell you who God is and what He looks like, because no one knows. But if you ask: What is God, I can say: Look around you at the flowers, the trees, the beasts, and at human beings, and then you will know what God is. This wonderful thing that lives and dies, that reproduces and that we call nature—that is God. He has made all this; you don't need to have any other idea of Him. God is men's name for this great miracle; they could just as well call it something else. Don't you agree with me, Cady?"

"Yes, I understand all that, I've thought about it myself. Sometimes, when the doctor in the hospital said to me: 'You're making good progress, I'm almost sure you'll get well,' I was so grateful, and—leaving out the doctor and the nurses, whom was I to be grateful to but God? But on the other hand, when I was in great pain, I thought that what I called God was Fate. So I kept going around in circles, and never came to any final conclusion. But when I asked myself, what do you actually believe, I was sure I believed in God. I often ask God for advice, so to speak, and when I do, I'm sure I get the one right answer. But, Hans, shouldn't that answer somehow come out of myself?"

"As I've told you, Cady, God created people and all living things just as they are. Our soul and our sense of justice come from Him. The answer you get to your questions comes from yourself, but also from God, because He made you as you are."

"So you think God speaks to me through myself?"

"Yes, I do. And in speaking of these things, Cady, we have shown great confidence. Give me your hand as a sign that we shall always trust each other, and when one of us is in difficulty and would like to talk to someone about it, then both of us will know where to turn."

Cady gave him her hand, and so they sat for a long while, hand in hand, and a wonderful feeling of peace grew up inside them.

After this conversation about God, both Hans and Cady felt they had concluded a friendship that went much deeper than any outsider would have suspected. In the meantime Cady had got so used to writing everything that happened around her in her diary that soon she could describe her thoughts and feelings better there than anywhere else, except to Hans. One day she wrote:

"Though I have a real friend, I am not always happy

and cheerful. Do all people have such changing moods? But if I were always happy, perhaps I wouldn't think enough about all sorts of things that are certainly worth thinking about.

"Our conversation about God is still running through my head, and often, while reading in bed or in the woods, I think: How can God speak to me through myself? And then a whole discussion goes on inside me.

"I believe that God 'speaks through myself' because before sending people into the world He gives each one of them a little bit of Himself. It is that little bit of God in a person that makes the difference between good and evil and that provides the answer to His questions. That little bit is nature in the same sense as the growing of the flowers and the singing of the birds.

"But God also sowed passions and desires in men and in all men these desires are at war with justice.

"Who knows? Someday perhaps men will listen more to the 'little bit of God' that is called conscience than to their desires."

On September 3 the peace of the sanatorium was disturbed for the first time since Cady's arrival.

At one o'clock when she happened to be listening to the news on her headset, she was horrified when the A. and B. commentator announced that Minister Chamberlain had declared war on Germany. Cady had never taken an interest in politics, which was perfectly normal for a girl of fourteen, and anyway she wasn't moved by events in distant countries. But she had a vague idea that this declaration of war would affect her too someday. When the nurse served tea after lunch, she told the other patients the news.

All the patients who shared Cady's room were well on their way to recovery.

The day before the war broke out, a new lady had arrived in the ward. Her bed was next to Cady's. Except for "good morning" and "good night," Cady hadn't exchanged a word with this lady, but now, all by itself, or*

....

beside Cady had been silent.

Cady was aware of this and she noticed that tears were running down over the rather young-looking face, making it look sad and pitiful. She didn't dare to ask any questions for fear of disturbing the lady, who was deep in thought. A little later in the day, Cady was reading when she heard her neighbor sobbing. Quickly she laid her book down on her bedside table and asked in a soft voice: "Should I call the nurse? Don't you feel well?"

The woman looked up. Her face was stained with tears. For a moment she looked into Cady's eyes, then she said: "No, my child, never mind about me. My trouble is something that no nurses or medicine can help." At that Cady felt even sorrier for the woman. She looked so discouraged and dejected that after those words Cady couldn't rest: "Maybe I can help you," she said.

The woman, who had slumped down on her pillows, sat up again, dried her tears with her handkerchief, and gave Cady a friendly look. "I can see you're not asking out of curiosity," she said. "Though you're still very young, I'll tell you what's making me so miserable." Here she paused a moment, looked around her with unseeing eyes, and then went on: "My son, it's about my son. He's in England at boarding school, he was supposed to come home next month, and now, now . . ." Sobs prevented her from saying any more, but Cady filled in:

*Here, there was a break in the original manuscript—Trans.

"And now he can't come back anymore?" The answer was a faint nod: "Who knows how long this war will go on and what will happen over there. I don't believe all this talk about its being over in a few months. A war always lasts longer than people expect."

"But so far there's been no fighting except in Poland. You mustn't worry so. After all, your son is being taken care of." Though Cady knew nothing about the boy, she felt she had to make some answer to the woman's words of discouragement. But the woman didn't seem to hear her. "After every war," she went on, "people say never again, it was so terrible, it must never be allowed to happen again, but people always have to start fighting each other, and that's how it will always be, as long as humans live and breathe they will always quarrel and whenever they are at peace they will go looking for something to fight about."

"I don't know, I've never been through a war, and . . . but we're not at war, so far it doesn't affect us. Of course what you tell me about your son is a shame, but when the war is over I'm sure you'll be reunited in good health. But . . . wait a minute. What's to prevent your son from coming now? Travel between Holland and England hasn't been stopped. Just ask the doctor, he's sure to know. If your son leaves soon, he'll get home all right." Never had Cady seen such a sudden change in a face: "Do you really think so, I'd never thought of that; here comes the nurse, I'll ask her."

The nearest nurse came over at a sign from Cady and her neighbor. "Sister," the woman asked, "do you know if communications between Holland and England have been cut?"

"Not that I know of. Are you going to England?"

"No, that's not why I ask. Thank you very much, Sister."

After giving Cady another grateful look, the woman turned around and began to think out what she would write to her son.

It was a hard time for the Jews. The fate of many would be decided in 1942. In July they began to round up boys and girls and deport them. Luckily Cady's girl friend Mary seemed to have been forgotten. Later it wasn't just the young people, no one was spared. In the fall and winter Cady went through terrible experiences. Night after night she heard cars driving down the street, she heard children screaming and doors being slammed. Mr. and Mrs. Van Altenhoven looked at each other and Cady in the lamplight, and in their eyes the question could be read: "Whom will they take tomorrow?"

One evening in December, Cady decided to run over to Mary's house and cheer her up a little. That night the noise in the street was worse than ever. Cady rang three times at the Hopkens's and when Mary came to the front of the house and looked cautiously out of the window, she called out her name to reassure her. Cady was let in. The whole family sat waiting in gym suits, with packs on their backs. They all looked pale and didn't say a word when Cady stepped into the room. Would they sit there like this every night for months? The sight of all these pale, frightened faces was terrible. Every time a door slammed outside, a shock went through the people sitting there. Those slamming doors seemed to symbolize the slamming of the door of life.

At ten o'clock Cady took her leave. She saw there was no point in her sitting there, there was nothing she could do to help or comfort these people, who already seemed to be in another world. The only one who kept her courage up a little was Mary. She nodded to Cady from time to time and tried desperately to get her parents and sisters to eat something.

Mary took her to the door and bolted it after her. Cady started home with her little flashlight. She hadn't taken five steps when she stopped still and listened; she heard steps around the corner, a whole regiment of soldiers. She couldn't see much in the darkness, but she knew very well who was coming and what it meant. She flattened herself against a wall, switched off her light, and hoped the men wouldn't see her. Then suddenly one of them stopped in front of her, brandishing a pistol and looking at her with threatening eyes and a cruel face. "Come!" That was all he said, and immediately she was roughly seized and led away.

"I'm a Christian girl of respectable parents," she managed to say. She trembled from top to toe and wondered what this brute would do to her. At all costs she must try to show him her identity card.

"What do you mean respectable? Let's see your card."

Cady took it out of her pocket.

"Why didn't you say so right away?" the man said as he looked at it. *"So ein Lumpenpack!"* Before she knew it she was lying on the street. Furious over his own mistake, the German had given the "respectable Christian girl" a violent shove. Without a thought for her pain or anything else, Cady stood up and ran home.

After that night a week passed before Cady had a chance to visit Mary. But one afternoon she took time off, regardless of her work or other appointments. Before she got to the Hopkens's house she was as good as sure she wouldn't find Mary there, and, indeed, when she came to the door, it was sealed up.

Cady was seized with despair. "Who knows," she thought, "where Mary is now?" She turned around and went straight back home. She went to her room and slammed the door. With her coat still on, she threw herself down on the sofa, and thought and thought about Mary.

Why did Mary have to go away when she, Cady, could stay here? Why did Mary have to suffer her terrible fate when *she* was left to enjoy herself? What difference was there between them? Was she better than Mary in any way? Weren't they exactly the same? What crime had Mary committed? Oh, this could only be a terrible injustice. And suddenly she saw Mary's little figure before her, shut up in a cell, dressed in rags, with a sunken, emaciated face. Her eyes were very big, and she looked at Cady so sadly and reproachfully. Cady couldn't stand it anymore, she fell on her knees and cried and cried, cried till her whole body shook. Over and over again she saw Mary's eyes begging for help, help that Cady knew she couldn't give her.

"Mary, forgive me, come back . . ."

Cady no longer knew what to say or to think. For this misery that she saw so clearly before her eyes there were no words. Doors slammed in her ears, she heard children crying and in front of her she saw a troop of armed brutes, just like the one who had pushed her into the mud, and in among them, helpless and alone, Mary, Mary who was the same as she was.

PERSONAL REMINISCENCES
AND ESSAYS

Do You Remember?

REMINISCENCES OF MY SCHOOL DAYS

July 7, 1943

Do you remember? I spend happy hours talking about school, the instructors, our adventures, and—boys. When we still were part of ordinary, everyday life, everything was just marvelous. That one year in the Lyceum was sheer bliss for me; the teachers, all that they taught me, the jokes, the prestige, the romances, and the adoring boys.

Do you remember the day I came home from midtown, and there was a package in the mailbox, marked "D'un ami—R."? It couldn't have come from anyone but Rob. Wrapped in the little parcel was a breastpin worth at least two and one-half guilders, and ultramodern. Rob's father dealt in such things. I wore it two days, and then it broke.

Do you remember how Lies and I betrayed the class? We had a French test. I was pretty well prepared, but not Lies. She copied everything from me and I peeked at her work—to improve it! Though Lies' paper was a trifle better than mine, probably through the help I had given her, the teacher decided to give us both a big fat zero. Great indignation! We went to the headmaster to complain and set things straight. At the end of the conference, Lies blurted out, "But, mind you, sir, the entire class had open books under the desks!" The head promised not to punish the class, provided that all who had copied their work would raise their hands when asked about it. Ten hands, not even half the true number, went up. A day or two later, we were unexpectedly given the French test all over again. Lies and I were "cut dead" as traitors. Pretty soon I found myself unable to endure this treatment, and I wrote a long, pleading letter to Class 16 II, begging forgiveness. In two weeks, the whole thing was forgotten.

The letter was about as follows:

To the pupils of Class 16 II,

Anne Frank and Lies Goosens herewith offer the pupils of Class 16 II their sincere apologies for the cowardly betrayal in connection with the French test.

It was an unpremeditated, thoughtless act, and we admit without hesitation that we are the only ones who should have been punished. We think that anyone, in anger, might let a word or sentence slip that carries unpleasant consequences, but that was never intended to cause any harm. We hope that 16 II will regard the incident in that light and repay evil with good. Nothing can be done about it, and the two guilty ones can't undo their misdeed.

We wouldn't write this letter if we were not genuinely sorry. We ask those who have "cut" us until now to reconsider, for, after all, our act was not so heinous that we have to be looked upon as criminals for all eternity. We beg those who cannot get over our mistake to give us a thorough scolding or, if they prefer, ask us to perform some service which, if at all possible, we shall carry out.

We trust that all of the pupils in Class 16 II will forget the affair.

Anne Frank and
Lies Goosens

Do you remember how Pim told Rob in the tram that Anne was much prettier than Denise, especially when she smiled, and how Sanne, who was also a passenger, overheard this and repeated it to me? And that Rob answered, "Your nostrils are much too wide, Pim!"

Do you remember that Maurice wanted to call on Father to ask him if he could keep company with his daughter?

Do you remember that Rob and Anne Frank carried on a busy correspondence while Rob was sick in the hospital?

Do you remember how Sam pursued me on his bike and wanted to ride hand-in-hand with me?

Do you remember how Bram kissed me on the cheek when I gave him my solemn promise not to tell a soul about the goings-on between him and Suzy?

Oh how I wish that those happy, carefree days could come again!

The Flea

We've been having another calamity here, Mouschi's fleas. We didn't know cat fleas could get on people; but they can.

Yesterday I caught one on the upper part of my leg, then ten minutes later one farther down, and in the evening on Dussel's bed there was another running around on my leg. He slipped through my fingers, the critters are so terribly nimble. This morning when I was dressing in front of the cupboard another of those marvels jumped up on me. I'd never seen a flea that could run and jump. I caught him and pretty near crushed him, but Mr. Flea managed to get away. I sighed and took my clothes off again, and examined by naked boddy* and my clothes until I found the flea in my panties. Less than a second later his head was off.

*Misspelled in the original—Trans.

The Battle of the Potatoes

Wednesday, August 4, 1943

After about three months of peace, interrupted by occasional bickering, there was a big fight today. It happened while we were peeling potatoes early in the morning, and no one expected it. I'll give the gist of the argument; I couldn't keep up with it all, because everybody was talking at once.

Mrs. Van Daan started it (as usual) by saying that anybody who didn't help with the potato peeling in the morning would have to help in the afternoon. Nobody answered, and that didn't suit the Van Daans at all because a minute later Mr. Van Daan said the best way would be for everyone to peel his own potatoes, except Peter, because potato peeling wasn't suitable work for boys. (You see his brand of logic!)

And Mr. Van Daan went on: "I also fail to see why the men should always help; that's a very unfair distribution of labor; why should one do a lot more work for the community than the others?" At that point Mother stepped in, because she saw where the discussion was heading: "Aha, Mr. Van Daan, I see what you're getting at, you're going to say the children don't work enough. Don't you realize that when Margot doesn't help, Anne does, and vice versa? Peter doesn't help either, but in his case you think it unnecessary. Well, I find it unnecessary for the girls!"

Then Mr. Van Daan barked and Mrs. Van Daan spluttered, Dussel tried to calm them down, and Mommy shouted. The confusion was frightful, and there was poor little me, watching our supposedly "wise parents" literally at each other's throats.

The words flew thick and fast, Mrs. Van Daan accused Dussel of playing a double game (I think so too), Mr. Van Daan said something to Mother about community spirit, and said he worked so hard they should have pity on him. Then he suddenly started shouting: "It would make more sense for the children to help a little more instead of always sitting there with their noses stuck in books; there's no need for girls to learn so much!" (Modern, isn't he?) Mother said pretty calmly that she couldn't bring herself to feel sorry for Van Daan.

Then he started in again: "Why don't the girls ever carry the potatoes upstairs and why don't they ever get hot water, they're not all that weak." "You're crazy," Mother shouted suddenly, and that kind of frightened me, I wouldn't have thought she'd dare.

The rest doesn't really matter; nothing much came of it. Margot and I were appointed housemaids to the Secret Annex. Here a vulgar expression comes to mind. "You can kiss my . . ." Because naturally nothing of the kind will happen.

Van Daan also had the effrontery to say that Margot's washing up morning and noon for a whole year was no work at all.

When Father heard what had happened, he wanted to run upstairs and give Van Daan a good piece of his mind, but Mother thought it better to tell the man that if everyone should only take his own chestnuts out of the fire, then everyone should live on his own money.

My conclusion is this: the whole fuss is typical of the Van Daans, always warming up the same old slops. If Father weren't much too good to such people, he could remind them that we and the others literally saved their lives. In a labor camp they'd have to do worse things than peel potatoes . . . or even hunt cat fleas.

Villains!

Who are the villains here! Real villains! The Van Daans.

What's the trouble now?

I'm going to tell you.

It's the honest truth that we've got all these fleas in the house because of the Van Daans' indifference. For months we warned them: "Take your cat to the exterminator," we said. The answer was always: "Our cat has no fleas."

When the fleas were only too plainly proven and the itch kept us awake at night, Peter, who simply felt sorry for the cat, took a look, and true enough the fleas jumped straight in his face. He went to work, combed the cat with Mrs. Van Daan's fine comb, and brushed it with our one and only brush. What came to light?

At least a hundred fleas!

We asked Koophuis for advice, and the next day we put a disgusting green powder on everything. It didn't help. Then we got a spray gun with a kind of flea-Flit. Father, Dussel, Margot, and I were busy for a long time; we rubbed and swept and scrubbed and sprayed. Everything was full of it, clothes, blankets, floors, sofas, every nook and cranny; nothing was left unflitted.

Upstairs, too, Peter's room. The Van Daans thought there was no need for it in their room. We urged them to do at least their clothing, blankets, and chairs. They said they would. Everything was taken up to the attic and supposedly sprayed. Don't you believe it! The Franks are easy to fool. Nothing was done, there was no smell.

The excuse was: "The Flit smell would spoil our provisions."

Conclusion: They're to blame for bringing the fleas here. We get the stink, the itch and the bother.

Mrs. Van Daan can't stand the smell at night. Mr. Van Daan pretends to spray, but he brings the chairs, blankets, etc. back again unsprayed. Just let the Franks stifle in their fleas.

My First Day at the Lyceum

August 11, 1943

With a lot of fuss, talk, and planning, things were finally fixed so that I could register at the Lyceum and—without an entrance exam! I was a poor student in every subject, but particularly in math, and I trembled as I thought of the geometry course that stared me in the face.

At the end of September, the mail brought the long-awaited letter announcing the date in October on which I was to report at the Lyceum. That day it rained cats and dogs, and it was impossible to go by bike. So I used the tram, together with plenty of others.

There was a big crowd at the school; groups of boys and girls stood about, chatting; some walked from one group to another, recognizing friends and acquaintances, and asking, "What class are you in?"

Aside from Lies Goosens, I hadn't discovered a single person I knew who would become a classmate, and that situation didn't strike me as very pleasant. The school doors opened, and in our classroom we were welcomed by a gray teacher with a mouse face, who wore a long dress and flat-heeled shoes.

She stood there rubbing her hands as she watched the hubbub in front of her and made the usual announcements. The teacher called and checked the names of the students, told us what books had to be ordered, and discussed some other details. Then we were dismissed and could go home again.

To tell the truth, I was deeply disappointed; I had expected at least to see the schedule and—to meet the director. I did see, in one of the halls, a jolly, fat little man with red cheeks, who, smiling at everyone who passed, stood talking with another chap of the same height, who was thin, had a dignified face and silky hair, and wore spectacles. But I had no idea that the fat man was the building superintendent, and the thin one the director.

Back home I gave an excited report of my experiences, but, to be honest, I knew as much of the school, the instructors, the children, and the schedule as I did before I left.

School started a week later. Again the rain came down in buckets, but I insisted on going by bike. Mother packed a cover-all in my schoolbag so that, in heaven's name, I shouldn't get drenched, and off I went.

Margot rides her bike at a furious clip, and in a couple of minutes I was so out of breath that I begged her to slow down a little. Another few minutes and the heavy rain changed into a regular cloudburst. Mindful of Mother's cover-all, I stopped and, with much difficulty, put on that unflattering garment. I remounted my bike, but soon the pace proved too fast for me again, and once more I asked Margot to take it easy. Very much out of sorts, she said that in the future she'd prefer to ride by herself; no doubt she was afraid of being late. But we reached the school with time to spare and, after parking the bikes, we stood chatting for a while in the shelter of the arcade that leads to the Amstel River.

We entered school on the dot of eight-thirty. Just inside the entrance there was a big sign announcing that about twenty students had to change classrooms. I was included, and I was told to move to Class 16 II. This meant that I would belong to a group in which I knew a few boys and girls, but Lies was to remain in 12 I.

When I was given the desk at the very bottom of the class, behind girls much bigger than myself, I felt lonely and forsaken. In the second hour I raised my hand and asked to be moved to another spot, as I could see very little unless I fairly hung into the aisle.

My request was granted immediately, and I picked up my things and moved. The third hour was gym, and the teacher seemed so nice that I asked her to try to have Lies transferred to my room. How the dear lady did it I will never know, but the next hour, in walked Lies and was given the desk beside mine.

Now I was reconciled to the school—the school where I was to have so much fun and learn such a lot. Full of courage, I paid close attention to what the geography man was telling us.

A Lecture in Biology

August 11, 1943

Rubbing her hands, she walks into the room; rubbing her hands, she sits down; rubbing her hands, rubbing her hands, rubbing her hands.

Miss Riegel of Biology—small, gray, with gray-blue eyes, a big nose and a mouse face. In her wake, someone carries a map and the skeleton.

She takes her place behind the stove, still rubbing her hands, and begins the lesson. First she questions the students on their homework, then she lectures. Oh, she knows a lot, does Miss Riegel, and she is a clever lecturer, starting with fish and ending with reindeer. Her favorite topic, according to Margot, is propagation, which surely must be so because she is an old maid.

Suddenly she is interrupted; a small wad of paper flies through the air and lands on my desk.

"What have you there?" she asks in an accent that shows she hails from The Hague.*

*The setting of Anne's tales is, of course, Amsterdam. To the inhabitants of that city, the manner of speech of the people from The Hague sounds affected—Trans.

"I don't know, Miss Riegel."

"Come here, and bring that piece of paper with you."

I rise timidly and take the note to the front.

"Who is that from?"

"I don't know, Miss Riegel; I haven't read it."

"Ah, so we'll first attend to that."

She unfolds the note and shows me its content—the single word "traitor." I turn red. She looks at me.

"Now do you know who sent it?"

"No, Miss Riegel."

"You are lying."

I feel myself getting flaming red and stare at the teacher with what I know are flashing eyes, but I don't say a word.

"Tell me who wrote that note!" says Miss Riegel, addressing the class. "Whoever did it, raise your hand!"

Way back in the room a hand is raised. Just as I thought—it was Rob.

"Rob, come here!"

Rob now faces the teacher.

"Why did you write that note?"

Silence.

"Do you know, Anne, what it means?"

"Yes, Miss Riegel."

"Explain!"

"Can't I do it some other time? It is a long story."

"No. Explain!"

I tell her about the French test and the zeros Lies and I got for cheating, and the way we betrayed the class.

"A pretty story! And Rob, did you think it necessary to give Anne your opinion during a lecture? And Anne—I simply don't believe that you didn't know where that note came from. Sit down, both of you!"

I was furious. At home I told the whole miserable story in detail. Some weeks later, I thought I had a justified complaint about the grade Miss Riegel had given me on my report card, and I asked Father to talk to her about it. He came back without an improved mark, but with the information that, by mistake, he had called the teacher Miss Riggle throughout the interview. He further reported that she thought Anne Frank a very sweet girl, and had no recollection of the dear child ever having lied to her!

A Geometry Lesson

He's impressive as he stands before the class—a big, strong old man, his bald dome ringed with a wreath of gray. He always wears a gray suit and an old-fashioned high collar, its tips bent outward. He speaks with a peculiar accent; he often mutters and as often smiles. He is quite patient with those who do their best, but loses his temper in dealing with the lazy ones.

Of the ten children questioned, nine give unsatisfactory answers. He takes endless trouble in explaining, clarifying the problems; he reasons with the pupils so that they, themselves, may find the answers. He is fond of posing riddles and, after class, likes to talk of the days when he was president of one of the biggest soccer clubs in the country.

But Mijnheer Heesing and I were often at loggerheads, and always because—yes, because of my talking habit. In three lessons I got six reprimands. This was too much for the instructor, who, by way of remedy, prescribed an essay of two pages. It was handed in at the next lesson, and Mijnheer Heesing, who could take a joke, laughed as he read it and seemed particularly amused by this paragraph:

"I must, indeed, try hard to control the talking habit, but I'm afraid that little can be done, as my case is hereditary. My mother, too, is fond of chatting, and has handed this weakness down to me. Until now, she hasn't succeeded in getting it under control."

I had been told to write my essay under the title, "A Chatterbox."

But at the next lesson, I again was tempted to whisper a few remarks to my neighbor, and—Mijnheer Heesing took his little notebook and jotted down, "Miss Anne Frank: An essay entitled, 'An Incorrigible Chatterbox.' "

This piece of prose, too, was duly delivered. In Mijnheer Heesing's next lecture, however, I repeated my misdeed, and the instructor wrote in his little book, "Miss Anne Frank: An essay of two pages, entitled, ' "Quack, quack," said Mrs. Quackenbush.' "

What would you have thought in my place? It was pretty clear to me that Mijnheer Heesing was having a little joke; otherwise, he would surely have given me some stiff geometry problems to do. So I decided to answer his joke with a joke of my own and, with the help of Sanne Houtman, I wrote the "essay" in rhyme. Here is a part of it:

They cried, "Peep-peep" and "Quack-quack-quack."
"Quack, quack," said Mrs. Quackenbush,
As she called her big, big brood;
They waddled as fast as ever they could
And gave each other many a push

In their rush to reach their mother's wings.
"Oh, Mama, we hope you have some bread,
For all of us are nearly dead!"
They were very hungry, the poor things.
"Yes, sure," said Mama, "I have your lunch,
Eat this, and I will give you more;
To get it, I had to go ashore,
But, as you see, it was quite a hunch.
I had to steal it, but you be fair,
And each take his honest part."
The little ducklings were pretty smart,
And obeyed the mother then and there.
In doing it, they made a rumpus;
They cried, "Peep-peep" and "Quack-quack-quack."
But who was that with a ruffled back?
An angry swan! Oh, Heaven, help us!

—Etc., etc.

Heesing read it; read it aloud to the class, also read it to some other student groups, and gave in. From then on, we were good friends; he paid no further attention to my chattering, and never punished me again.

P.S. The long and short of it is that my math teacher was a very decent sort. The nickname "Mrs. Quackenbush" has stuck to me, and I have Mijnheer Heesing to thank for it.

Roomers or Subtenants

When we had to make up our minds to rent our big back room, it came as a hard blow, because none of us was used to having paying strangers in the house.

But when times are hard, when taking in roomers becomes a necessity, you have to swallow your pride and a good deal more. Which is just what we did. The big bedroom was cleaned out and refurnished with a few extra pieces that we had; but that wasn't nearly enough for a high-class bed-sitting room. So my father went out and poked around at all the auctions and public sales and came home today with one little thing and tomorrow with another.

Three weeks later we had a beautiful wastebasket and a lovely tea table, but we still needed two armchairs and a decent cupboard. My father went out again, and this time as a special attraction he took me along with him. Arrived at the auction, we sat down on wooden benches with some worn-out buyers and awful-looking characters and waited, waited, waited.

We could have waited until the next day, because on the day when we were there only porcelain was being auctioned off.

Disappointed, we went home, and next day we came back for another try, though without much hope. But this time we had better luck, and my father actually got hold of a fine oak cupboard and two leather club chairs.

By way of celebrating the new furniture and the roomers we hoped would arrive soon, we treated ourselves to a cup of tea and a piece of cake. Then we went cheerfully home. But hold on, when the cupboard and chairs were delivered next day and put in the room, my mother found the funniest little holes in the cupboard; my father examined it and . . . true enough, the cupboard was full of woodworms. Such things aren't marked down on paper and neither can you see them in a dark auction room.

After that discovery, we inspected the chairs, and they too were full of worms.

We called up the auction rooms and asked them to take the things away as soon as possible. They came all right and my mother sighed with relief as she watched the auction furniture going out the door. My father sighed too, but that was because of the money he had lost on this proposition.

A few days later my father met a friend who had some extra furniture, and was glad to let us have a few pieces until we could find something better. So at last our problem was solved.

Then we made up an ad and put it in the window of the corner bookstore, and paid for a whole week.

People soon came to look at the room. The first was an old gentleman, who wanted a room for his unmarried son. Everything was almost settled, when the son put in a few

words and what he said was so crazy that my mother began seriously to suspect that he had a screw loose. And
she was quite right, because the old gentleman admitted
rather sheepishly that his son wasn't quite right in the
head. My mother showed them the door as quickly as possible. Dozens of people came and went, until one day we
opened the door to a fat little man, who was willing to
pay and didn't ask for very much, so we took him. That
gentleman really gave us more pleasure than trouble.
Every Sunday he brought chocolate for the children and
cigarettes for the grown-ups, and more than once he took
us all to the movies. After living with us for one and a half
years, he took an apartment of his own with his mother
and sister. Once when he came to see us later on, he said
he had never had such a good time as with us. Again the
ad was hung up in the shop window and again big and
little, young and old people rang the bell. One was a
fairly young lady with a kind of Salvation Army hat, so
then and there we started calling her "Salvation Army Josephine." We took her, but she wasn't as pleasant a
roomer as the fat gentleman. In the first place, she was an
awful slob, she left things lying around all over the place,
and in the second place, which was worse, she had a fi-
ancé who often got drunk and we didn't like that in the
house. One night, for instance, we were all woken up by
the bell; father went down to see, and who should he run
into but this lout, as drunk as a lord, and he kept pounding my father on the back and shouting: "We're good
friends, aren't we! Oh yes, we're good friends!" Bang!
My father slammed the door in his face.

When the war broke out in May 1940, we gave her notice and rented the room to a friend, a young man of
about thirty, who was engaged to be married.

He was very nice, but he too had a drawback: he was

terribly spoiled. Once in the cold winter days, when we all had to scrimp on electricity, he complained bloody murder about the cold. Which was a shameful exaggeration, because his room was the warmest in the house.

But you have to be patient with roomers, so we gave him permission to use his electric heater for an hour now and then. And what was the upshot? All day long he kept his heater on "hot." We begged and pleaded with him to be a little more economical, but it didn't help. The electric meter went up something awful, and one fine day my dauntless mother unscrewed the fuse and disappeared for the afternoon. She put the blame on his stove, said it put too much of a strain on the fuse, and after that the young man had to sit in the cold.

All the same, he too stayed with us for one and a half years; then he moved out and got married.

Again the room was empty and my mother was going to put in an ad when a friend called up and made us take a divorced man, who was in urgent need of a room. He was a big tall man of thirty-five with glasses, most unprepossessing to look at. We didn't want to disappoint our friend, so we rented the room to this gentleman. He too was engaged and the girl often came to our house. It was almost time for the wedding when they quarreled and head over heels he married a different girl.

About that time we moved, and then we were rid of our roomers (for good, I hope)!

Dreams of Movie Stardom

December 24, 1943

(This was written as a "secret" answer to the questions of Mrs. Van Daan, who never tired of asking me why I didn't want to become a movie star.)

I was seventeen, an attractive girl with flirtatious eyes and a wealth of dark curls—a teen-ager filled with ideals, illusions, and daydreams. In one way or another, the day would come when my name would be a household word and my picture would occupy a place of honor in the memory book of every damp-eyed bobby-soxer.

The questions of how I was to achieve fame and in what field bothered me very little. When I was fourteen I used to think, "That will come in good time," and when I was seventeen I thought so still. My parents were not aware of my grandiose plans, and I was foxy enough to keep them to myself. It seemed to me that I'd be better off, should I ever become a celebrity, to experience things in private before sharing my adventures with Father and Mother. I suspected that they might not be overly enthusiastic about such a turn of events.

Let no one think that I took those daydreams of mine very seriously, or that I had thoughts for nothing else. On the contrary, I was always industrious in school and, besides, did much reading for pleasure. At fifteen I had finished one of our three-year high schools. Now, mornings, I attended a school that specialized in teaching foreign languages, and in the afternoons, I did my homework or played tennis. One day (it was autumn) I was home cleaning up a closet, when, amid a pile of assorted discarded stuff, I came upon a shoe box, with the words MOVIE STARS written in large letters on the lid. I remembered that my parents had ordered me to throw this box out, and that I had hidden it carefully so nobody would find it.

Curious, I lifted the lid, took out the many little packages inside, and loosened the elastic bands in which each was wrapped. I got so fascinated looking once more at all the made-up faces, that I was startled when, a couple of hours later, someone tapped me on the shoulder to ask me to come to tea. I was sitting on the floor, surrounded by little stacks of newspaper and magazine clippings.

Later, in straightening my room, I kept the movie-star box aside. That evening, I continued my examination and found something that impressed me so that I couldn't get it out of my mind.

This was an envelope filled with pictures of a family of movie actors, in which three daughters were stars. I came across the address of the girls, whose name was Lane. Then and there, I took a piece of paper and a pen and started writing a letter to the youngest of the sisters—Priscilla Lane.

Secretly, I mailed the letter, which was in English. In it I told Priscilla that I would love to have a photo of her, and also of both her sisters, and asked her to be good enough to answer me, as I was keenly interested in the family.

I waited more than two months and, though I didn't want to admit it to myself, I had lost hope of ever getting an answer to my letter. There was nothing surprising in this, for I realized that if the Lane girls answered the notes of all their admirers and sent photographs to them, all of their time would have to be devoted to their correspondence. But just then my father one morning handed me a letter addressed to "Miss Anne Franklin."

I hastily opened and read it. My family were very curious and, after I had told them of my letter, I read Priscilla's aloud. She wrote that she would not send photos before she knew something more about me, but that she would be more inclined to do so if I would write her, in more detail, about myself and my family.

Truthfully, I wrote Priscilla that I was more interested in her personal life than in her film career. I wanted to know, among other things, if she went out much in the evening; if Rosemary had to work as much and as hard as she, etc., etc. Much later she asked me to call her by her nickname of "Pat." Priscilla seemed so pleased with my letters that she answered each one faithfully.

As the correspondence was, naturally, conducted in English, my parents couldn't object, as it obviously provided good practice for me. In her letters, Priscilla told me that she spent most of her days at the studio and gave me an idea of how she divided her time. She corrected my mistakes and mailed my letters back to me, on condition that I would return them again to her. Meanwhile she had sent me a big collection of photos.

Priscilla, who was twenty, was neither engaged nor married, which didn't disturb me in the least. I was immensely proud of my friend, the movie star.

So passed the winter. In late spring a letter came from the Lanes, in which Priscilla asked me if I would like to fly to the United States and spend two of the summer months as their guest. I jumped for joy, but I hadn't reckoned with the objections of my parents. I couldn't accept the invitation; it was impossible for me to travel alone to America; I didn't have enough clothes; I couldn't stay away that long, and all the other worried notions that occur to loving fathers and mothers on such occasions. But I had made up my mind to go to America, and go I must.

I reported all of the parental objections to Priscilla, and she answered each one to my satisfaction. First of all, I wouldn't have to travel alone. Priscilla's companion, who was visiting relatives of hers in The Hague, would take me with her to the States. As for my return trip to Holland, Priscilla would think of a chaperone when the time came.

My parents still objected: Neither I nor they really knew the Lane family, they said, and it was more than likely that I would feel entirely out of place in their home. They made me cross; it almost seemed as though they begrudged me this unusual opportunity. I pleaded that it would be almost an insult to decline such a cordial invitation. After they had received a charming and reassuring letter from Mrs. Lane, they finally decided the matter in my favor. I worked hard in the months of May and June, and when Priscilla wrote that her companion would arrive in Amsterdam on July 18, preparations for my voyage were completed.

On the eighteenth, Father and I went to the station to meet the lady. Priscilla had sent me her photograph, and I recognized her at once among the many detraining passengers. Miss Halwood was a small woman with graying blond hair, who talked much and rapidly. She looked like a sweet person.

Father, who had once been in America and spoke good English, conversed with Miss Halwood, and I ventured a remark now and then. It had been arranged that she would stay with us for a week. That week fairly flew by, and scarcely a day had passed before Miss Halwood and I were friends.

On July 25, I was so excited that I couldn't swallow a single bite of my breakfast. But Miss Halwood, an experienced traveler, gave no sign of agitation. The entire family saw us off at Schiphol Airport, and finally, finally, my trip to America had begun.

We arrived in the neighborhood of Hollywood on the evening of the fifth day. Priscilla and her sister Rosemary, her senior by one year, met us. As I was somewhat tired from the trip, we drove to a hotel near the airport. After breakfast the next morning, we stepped again into the car, which was driven by Rosemary.

In slightly more than three hours, we reached the Lane house, where I was cordially received.

Mrs. Lane showed me to my room, which was really a charming small apartment with a balcony. This, then, was to be my home for the next two months.

It was not difficult to feel at ease in the hospitable Lane home. Much work and much fun were the daily routine; the three famous young stars, by the way, helped their mother more than I, an ordinary teen-ager, ever did. I soon got used to speaking English. Priscilla was free during the first two weeks of my stay and showed me much of the beautiful surroundings. Nearly every day we went to the beach, and I gradually became acquainted with people of whom I had heard or read. One of Priscilla's intimate friends was Madge Bellamy, who often went along with us on our sight-seeing jaunts.

Nobody would have judged Priscilla to be older than myself; she treated me as a girl of her own age. When her free fortnight was up, she had to go back to the Warner Brothers studio and—oh, joy!—I was allowed to go with her. I visited her in her dressing room and saw Priscilla making tests.

She finished early that first day and showed me around the studio. "Anne," she said after a while, "I just got a wonderful idea. Tomorrow morning you go to the office where pretty girls apply for jobs and ask the man in charge if there is anything you could do. Just in fun, of course."

"Yes, I'd like that," I said. Next day, I really did go to that office. It was a terribly busy place; the girls stood queued up in the hall. I joined the line and in half an hour I was inside the office. But that didn't mean that it was my turn; there were still many girls ahead of me. Again I waited, this time about two hours. A bell rang—this was for me!—and bravely I stepped into the inner office, where a middle-aged man was seated behind a desk. He greeted me in a standoffish manner. Asking my name and address, he seemed surprised that I was a guest of the Lanes. Finished with those questions, he took another good look at me and asked, "I suppose that you want to be a film star?"

"Yes, sir, if I have the talent."

He pushed a button, and in walked a smartly dressed girl, who asked me, with a gesture rather than in words, to follow her. She opened a door, and the sharp light in the room made me blink my eyes. A young man behind an intricate apparatus gave me a friendlier greeting than the one I'd had before and told me to sit on a high stool. He took several pictures, then rang for the girl, and I was led back to the older man. He promised to send me word whether or not I should return to the studio.

Encouraged, I found my way back to the Lane house. A week later I received a note from Mr. Harwick (Priscilla had told me his name). He wrote that the photos had come out very well, and asked me to come to his office at three o'clock the next afternoon.

Now, armed with an invitation, I was admitted at once. Mr. Harwick asked me if I would pose for a manufacturer of tennis rackets. The job was for just one week, but after I had been told what I would be paid, I gladly consented. Mr. Harwick called the tennis man, whom I met that same afternoon.

Next day I made my appearance at a photo studio, where I was to go every day for a week. I had to change clothes in minutes; I had to stand, sit, and smile continuously; walk up and down, change clothes again, look pretty, and put on fresh make-up. At night I was so exhausted that I had to drag myself to bed. On the third day it hurt me to smile, but I felt that I must keep faith with my manufacturer.

When I came home on the evening of the fourth day, I must have looked so ill that Mrs. Lane forbade me to return to the job. She herself called the man, and got him to excuse me.

I was deeply grateful. Undisturbed, I hugely enjoyed the rest of my unforgettable vacation. As for dreams of movie stardom, I was cured. I had had a close look at the way celebrities live.

Sunday

Sunday, February 20, 1944

What happens during the week in other people's houses happens on Sunday here in the Secret Annex. While other people put on their fine clothes and go walking in the sunshine, we here are scrubbing, sweeping, and washing clothes.

8 o'clock: With no consideration for the late sleepers, Dussel gets up at 8. He goes to the bathroom, then downstairs, then up again, and then in the bathroom he does a big washing that takes a whole hour.

9:30: The stoves are lit. The blackout curtains are taken down and the Van Daans go into the bathroom. One of my Sunday morning tortures is that lying in bed I have to look straight at Dussel's back when he's praying. You'll all laugh when I tell you how awful it is to watch Dussel pray. It's not that he cries or gets sentimental, not at all, but he has this way of seesawing from his heels to his toes and back again for a quarter of an hour, ah yes, a quarter of an hour. Back and forth, back and forth, on and on. If I don't shut my eyes, it makes my head spin.

10:15: The Van Daans whistle, the bathroom is free. On our floor the first sleepy faces rise from their pillows. Then everything goes fast, fast, fast. Margot and I take turns helping with the washing. Seeing it's bitter cold down below, we're glad to be wearing long trousers and head scarves. Meanwhile, Father is busy in the bathroom; at 11 Margot (or I) goes into the bathroom, and then we're all clean again.

11:30: Breakfast. I won't say any more about that, because there's enough talk about food without my contribution.

12:15: Everybody does something different. Father in overalls gets down on his knees and brushes the carpet so hard that the room is cloaked in a big cloud of dust. Dussel makes the beds (all wrong, naturally!), meanwhile whistling the same old Beethoven violin concerto. Mother can be heard shuffling across the floor while she hangs up the washing.

Mr. Van Daan puts on his hat and disappears into the nether regions, usually followed by Peter and Mouschi. Mrs. Van Daan puts on a long apron, a black woolen vest and overshoes, ties a thick red woolen shawl around her head, takes a bundle of filthy washing under her arm and, after a well-rehearsed washerwoman's curtsy, also goes down to the washtubs.

Margot and I do the dishes and straighten the bedroom a little.

At a quarter to 1: When everything is dry and only the pots and pans are left, I go downstairs to dust and if I've done washing in the morning to clean the washtub.

1 o'clock: News.

Quarter past 1: One of us has his hair washed or cut. Then we all get busy peeling potatoes, hanging up washing, waxing the stairs, scrubbing the bathroom, etc., etc.

2 o'clock: After the Wehrmacht communiqué we wait for the music program and coffee and all is calm again. Who can tell why the grown-ups here have to sleep all the time? By 11 o'clock in the morning you see some of them yawning and often enough you hear them sighing: "Oh, if only I could stretch out for half an hour!"

It's really no joke between 2 and 4 in the afternoon to see nothing but sleepy faces wherever you go. In our room Dussel, in the living room Father and Mother and upstairs the Van Daans, who exchange sleeping places in the afternoon. Oh well, it can't be helped, maybe I'll understand when I'm as old as they are.

Anyway, they sleep even longer on Sunday. No point in going upstairs before 4:30 or 5, because until then they're all in dreamland.

The late afternoon is the same as on weekdays, except for the concert from 6 to 7 o'clock.

Once we've eaten and washed up, I'm happy because another Sunday is gone.

My First Article

February 22, 1944

Imagine that the subject of my first article knew that he was going to be used as "material"—wouldn't he turn red and ask, "Why me? What's so interesting about me?" Let me put the cards on the table: Peter is my subject, and now I'll tell how that occurred to me.

I wanted to write about somebody, and as I already had described most of the other people in the house, I thought of Peter. The boy always keeps himself in the background and, like Margot, never causes dissention.

If, toward evening, you knock on the door of his room and hear him call a soft "Come in!" you may be sure that, on opening the door, you'll find him looking at you through two of the steps of the ladder to the attic and saying, "So!" in a gentle, inviting tone.

His little room is—what is it really? I think it is a passage to the attic, very narrow, very drafty, but—he has turned it into a room. When he sits at the left of the ladder, there's surely no more than a yard's space between him and the wall. There stand his little table, laden, like ours, with books (a few steps of the ladder also hold some of his possessions) and a chair.

On the other side of the ladder, his bike hangs from the ceiling. Useless at present, it is carefully wrapped in brown paper, but a small chain, dangling from one of the pedals, is still visible. This corner is completed by a lamp with an ultramodern shade, made from a piece of cardboard covered with strips of paper.

I am still standing in the open door, and now I look in the other direction. Against the wall—that is, opposite Peter and behind the table—stands an old divan, covered with blue flowered stuff; the bedclothes have been hidden (but not quite successfully) behind it. Above the daybed hangs a lamp, the mate of the other one, and similarly decorated. A bit further on, there is a small bookcase filled, from top to bottom, with paper-covered books that could belong only to a boy. A hand mirror is fastened to the wall beside it. Probably because the owner didn't know where else to put it, a small tool chest stands on the floor. (I know from experience that anything in the way of a hammer, a knife, or a screw driver one may need, can be found in its depths.)

Near the bookcase, a shelf, covered with paper that once was white, was originally meant for such things as milk bottles, but has been converted into an annex of the library; it all but groans under the weight of books. The milk bottles have become neighbors of the tool chest, on the floor.

On the third wall hangs a wooden case that may have contained oranges or cherries, but that now serves as a cabinet for such articles as a shaving brush, a safety razor, a roll of plaster, a small bottle of laxative, etc. Beside the cabinet stands the prize exhibit of the Van Daan family's ingenuity—a closet made of cardboard, held together by two or three uprights of some sturdier material. In front of the closet there hangs a really handsome drape, which Peter, after much coaxing, got from his mother. The closet itself is filled with suits, overcoats, socks, shoes, and the like. The stuff massed on the top of the closet is so mixed up that I've never been able to recognize one single item.

The floor coverings of Mr. Van Daan, Jr., also are worth seeing. He has one small and two large genuine Persian rugs of such striking colors that everyone who enters the little room remarks on them. These pieces, which at one time must have cost a great deal, lie on a floor so shaky and irregular that one can't walk on it without the utmost caution.

Two of the walls are covered with green jute, and the other two are generously plastered with pictures of more or less beautiful movie stars and advertising posters. Grease and scorch spots should cause no surprise, for it is to be expected that, with so much stuff in a small space, something or other is bound to get dirty in a year and a half. The beamed ceiling, also, is no longer in good condition and, since there are leaks in the roof and Peter's room is in the attic, he has spread some sheets of cardboard to catch the drip. Innumerable water spots and rings show that this protection is far from adequate.

Now, I believe, I've gone all around the room; I have forgotten only the chairs. One of them is an old wooden armchair of Viennese design with perforated seat; number two is a white kitchen chair which Peter appropriated last year. He started to scrape off the paint, probably with the idea of giving it a fresh color, but he didn't have much luck and stopped. And so, half scraped off, part white, part black, and with only one rung (we used the other for a poker), the chair isn't very pretty. But, as has been said, the place is dark, and the poor wreck doesn't attract much attention.

The door to the kitchen steps is festooned with aprons; there are also a few hooks with dustcloths and a brush. After all this, everyone should know each nook and cranny of Peter's room, but not, of course, the inhabitant himself. And now it's the turn of the owner of all these glorious possessions.

There's a sharp difference in Peter's appearance on weekdays and Sundays. Weekdays he wears cover-alls, from which he rarely separates himself, as he objects to having the things washed too often. I can't imagine the reason for this attitude, except that he fears his favorite piece of apparel might wear out that way. At any rate, it just has been laundered, and its color—blue—is once more recognizable. Round his neck Peter wears a blue scarf, which apparently is just as dear to him as the cover-alls. A heavy, brown leather belt and white woolen socks complete his weekday attire. But on Sundays Peter's clothing may be said to undergo a rebirth. Then he wears a handsome suit, a fine pair of shoes, a shirt, a necktie— everything that belongs to a young man's nice wardrobe.

So much for Peter's appearance. As for the man himself, I have changed my opinion radically of late. I used to think him dumb and slow, but nowadays he is neither the one nor the other. Everybody agrees that he has grown into a fine young fellow. I know in my heart that he is honest and generous. He has always been modest and helpful, and I think that he is much more sensitive than people give him credit for. He has one preference that I shall never forget—the cats. Nothing is too much trouble where Mouschi or Moffi are concerned, and I do believe that those two sense that there isn't much love in his life and try to make up for it.

He's not afraid—on the contrary—and not as smart-alecky as other boys of his age. He isn't stupid, either, and has a remarkably good memory. That he is handsome I needn't say, for everyone who sees him knows that. His hair is wonderful—a wealth of fine brown curls. He has gray-blue eyes, and—describing faces has always been my weak point. After the war I'll paste his photo, together with those of the other people who were in hiding with us, in this book by way of illustration. That will save me the trouble of describing them.

The Sink of Iniquity

Don't worry, I'm not going to give you a list of examples to illustrate my title. My reason for picking this title is that I saw those words in a magazine yesterday (*C & T*, No. 8).

In what connection, you're sure to ask, and I'll answer you right away. The Sink of Iniquity was in a magazine in connection with some naked pictures in a movie, which the critic evidently thought indecent. I won't go so far as to say he wasn't right, but in the main I believe that people here in Holland tend to find fault with anybody who hasn't got quite enough clothes on.

This attitude is known as prudishness, and on the one hand there may be something good about it but on the other hand, if all children were taught that everything connected with nakedness is indecent, the upshot would be that the young people would start wondering: "My goodness, are they all completely cracked?"

And I can't help agreeing with them. Modesty and prudishness can go too far, and that is certainly the case in the Netherlands, if you consider how ridiculous it is that if you merely pronounce the word "naked" people stare at you from all sides as if you were the most improper person in the world.

You mustn't suppose that I'm one of those who want us to live like the cavemen or go running around in animal skins; not at all, I just want our lives to be a little freer, a little more natural, a little more informal. And now let me ask you a question. "Do you put clothes on flowers when you pick them? And do you never say anything about the way they look?"

I don't think we're so very different from nature. And since we people are a part of nature, why should we be ashamed of the way nature has dressed us?

Happiness

Before I begin my story, I'll tell quickly what has happened in my life so far.

I have lost my mother (I've really never known her), and my father hasn't much time for me. When my mother died, I was two years old; my father gave me into the care of a charming couple, with whom I remained five years. So I was seven when I was sent to boarding school. I stayed there until I was fourteen; then I was, happily, allowed to join my father. Now he and I live in a pension, and I go to the Lyceum. Nothing out of the ordinary happened to me until—until I met Jacques.

We became acquainted because he moved into our pension with his parents. First we saw each other a few times on the stairway; then, by chance, in the park, and after that we went several times for a walk in the woods.

From the first, Jacques impressed me as a splendid boy, perhaps a little shy and withdrawn, though that may have been the very quality that attracted me. Gradually, we had more dates together, and now we often visit one another in each other's rooms.

I had never had a close acquaintance with a boy before, and I was surprised to find him entirely different from the boys in my class, who were boisterous and boastful.

I began to think about Jacques, after thinking a good deal about myself. I knew that his parents didn't get along together and quarreled often, and I felt that this must disturb him very much, for a love of peace and quiet was one of his characteristics.

I am alone most of the time and often feel sad and lonely; it's probably because I miss my mother and because I've never had a real friend in whom I could confide. Jacques is in the same situation; he also had only superficial friends, and it seemed to me that he, too, needed someone to take into his confidence. But I couldn't get closer to him and we continued to talk about unimportant things.

But, one day, he came with an obviously made-up excuse, as I was sitting on a cushion on the floor, looking at the sky.

"Do I interrupt?" he asked.

"Certainly not," I said, turning toward him. "Sit down beside me, or don't you believe in dreaming?"

He stood by the window, leaning his forehead against the pane.

"Oh, yes," he said, "I dream a lot like this. Do you know what I call it? Taking a look at the history of the world."

"That's a fine way of putting it; I must remember it."

"Yes," he said, with the peculiar smile that always confused me a little, because I never knew exactly what it meant.

We talked again of trivial things, and after a while he left.

The next time he called on me, I happened to sit in the same spot, and he once more took up his place by the window. That day, the weather was magnificent; the sky was a deep blue (we were up so high that we couldn't see the houses, at least not I, from my spot on the floor); dewdrops clung to the bare branches of the chestnut tree in front of the house, and the sun turned each drop into a sparkling diamond as the branches slowly moved. Seagulls and other birds flew, chattering, past our window.

I don't know why it was, but neither of us could utter a word. Here we were, in the same room, not far from each other, but we scarcely saw one another anymore. We looked only at the sky, and talked to ourselves. I say "we," for I am sure that he felt as I did, and that he was making no more effort to break the silence than I.

Fifteen minutes—then he spoke. He said: "When you let beauty and peace sink into you, dissension and strife begin to look like sheer insanity. Everything that people make a fuss about becomes unimportant. And yet, I don't always feel this way."

He looked shyly at me, perhaps afraid that I might not understand him. I was delighted that he expected me to answer, that I finally had found a sympathetic person to whom I could tell my thoughts.

"Do you know what I always think?" I said. "That it is silly to fight with people about whom you feel indifferent. To differ with people for whom you care is another story. You are fond of them, and it hurts you more than it angers you when they provoke you."

"Do you really think so, too? But you don't quarrel much, do you?"

"No, but enough to know what it is like. The worst of it is that most people go alone through this world."

"What do you mean by that?" Jacques now was looking straight at me, but I decided to persist; perhaps I might be able to help him.

"I mean that most people, married or single, stand inwardly alone. They have no one with whom they can talk about all of their feelings and thoughts; and that is what I miss the most."

All Jacques said was, "It is the same with me."

We took another look at the sky. Then he said, "People who, as you put it, have no one to talk to, miss much, very much. And it is just that realization which so often depresses me."

"No, I don't agree. Nobody can help feeling depressed now and then, but there's no point in anticipating that you're going to be sad.

"You see, what you look for when you are depressed is happiness. No matter how much you miss someone to whom you could express your feelings, happiness, once you have found it and keep it in your heart, can never be lost."

"How did you find it?"

I got up. "Come along," I said, and I went ahead of him, up the stairs, to the attic. There was a storage space with a window. The house was unusually tall, and when we looked out of the window, we saw a great stretch of sky.

"Look," I said. "If you want to find happiness within yourself, you have to go outside on a day with much sun and a lovely blue sky. Or you could stand at a window such as this, and look at our city under the brilliant blue. Sooner or later, you will find it.

"Let me tell you what happened to me. I was in boarding school, which I never liked. The older I got, the more I disliked it. One free afternoon, I went alone for a walk on the moor. I sat down and dreamed for a while.

"When I looked up again, I realized that it was a glorious day. Until then, I had been so wrapped up in my own gloomy thoughts that I had paid no attention to it.

"From the moment that I saw and felt the beauty all around me, that little nagging inner voice stopped reminding me of my worries. I could no longer feel or think of anything but that this was beauty and this was truth.

"I sat there for about half an hour, and when I got up and walked back to that hateful school, I was no longer depressed. Everything impressed me as good and beautiful, the way it really was.

"Later I understood that, on that afternoon, I had for the first time found happiness within myself. I also realized that no matter what the circumstances, happiness is always there."

"And did it change you?" he asked.

"Yes, it did. I was content. Not always, mind you; I still grumbled from time to time, but I never was downright miserable again. I had learned that most sadness comes from self-pity, but that happiness comes from joy."

When I had finished, he was still looking out of the window and seemed lost in thought. Suddenly he turned and looked at me.

"I haven't found happiness yet," he said, "but I found something else—someone who understands me."

I knew what he meant. From then on, I was no longer alone.

Give

I wonder if any of the people sitting in warm, comfortable homes have any idea what it must be like to be a beggar? Have any of those "good, dear people" ever asked themselves about the lives of poor people or children around them? All right, everyone gives a beggar a few coppers now and then. But it is usually pushed hurriedly into his hands, and the door is closed with a bang. And what is more, the generous donor usually shudders at having to touch such a dirty hand. *Is it true, or isn't it?* And then people are surprised that beggars become so rude. Wouldn't anyone, who was treated more like a beast than a human being?

It is bad, very bad indeed, that in a country which claims to have good social laws and a high standard of culture people should treat each other in this way. Most of the well-to-do people regard a beggar as someone to be despised, dirty and uncared for, rude and uncivilized. But have any of them ever asked themselves how these poor wretches have become like this? Just compare your own children with these poor children. Whatever is the difference really? Your children are clean and tidy, the others dirty and uncared for. Is that all? Yes, that's really the only difference. But if a poor beggar's child were to receive good clothes and learn nice manners, then there wouldn't be any difference at all.

We are all born alike, they were helpless and innocent too. Everyone breathes the same air, a great many people believe in the same God! And yet, yet the difference can be so immeasurably great, because so many people have never realized where the difference really lies. Because if they had realized it, they would have discovered that there really wasn't any difference at all. Everyone is born the same, everyone has to die, and nothing remains of their worldly glory. Riches, power, and fame last only for a few years! Why do people cling so desperately to these transitory things? Why can't people who have more than they need for themselves give that surplus to their fellow citizens? Why should some people have such a hard time during their few years on this earth? But above all, let the gifts be given kindly and not just flung in their faces; everyone has the right to a friendly word! Why should one be nicer to a rich woman than to a poor one? Has anyone sorted out the difference in character between the two? The true greatness of a person does not lie in riches or power, but in character and goodness. Everyone is human, everyone has his faults and shortcomings, but everyone is born with a great deal that is good in him. And if one were to begin by encouraging the good, instead of smothering it, by giving poor people the feeling that they are human beings too, one would not even need money or possessions to do this.

Everything begins with the little things. For instance, don't only stand up in a tram for the rich mothers, no, remember the poor ones too. Say you are sorry if you step on a poor person's toes as you would for someone rich. People will always follow a good example; be the one to set the good example, then it won't be long before others follow. More and more people will become friendly and generous, until finally poor people will not be looked down upon anymore.

Oh, if only we were that far already, that our country and then Europe and finally the whole world would realize that people were really kindly disposed toward one another, that they are all equal and everything else is just transitory!

How lovely to think that no one need wait a moment, we can start now, start slowly changing the world! How lovely that everyone, great and small, can make their contribution toward introducing justice straightaway! Just as with so many things, most people seek justice in quite another quarter, they grumble because they receive so little of it themselves. Open your eyes, first make sure that you are always fair yourself! Give of yourself, give as much as you can! And you can always, always give something, even if it is only kindness! If everyone were to do this and not be as mean with a kindly word, then there would be much more justice and love in the world. Give and you shall receive, much more than you would have ever thought possible. Give, give again and again, don't lose courage, keep it up and go on giving! No one has ever become poor from giving! If you do this, then in a few generations no one will need to pity the beggar children anymore, because they will not exist!

There is plenty of room for everyone in the world, enough money, riches, and beauty for all to share! God has made enough for everyone! Let us all begin then by sharing it fairly.

Who Is Interesting?

Last week I was riding in the train on my way to see my aunt in Bussum. My plan was to enjoy myself in the train at least, because putting up with Aunt Josephine's company for a whole week is no fun at all.

So there I sat with my plan, but I was unlucky, because at first sight my companions didn't look very interesting or amusing. The little old woman who sat facing me was friendly enough, but not at all amusing, and neither was the distinguished gentleman next to her, who couldn't possibly have been pried loose from his newspaper, and the peasant woman on the other side didn't look much like a friendly chat. But I'd made up my mind to enjoy myself, and no one was going to stop me.

If necessary, I'd just have to pester somebody; well, in that case, I'd put the blame on Aunt Josephine's long skinny neck. After I'd mulled over my plan for ten or fifteen minutes, certainly looking no more amusing than my traveling companions, the train stopped at the first station and to my great joy a gentleman of about thirty got in, who looked interesting if not amusing.

Women in general are convinced that young men with graying hair at the temples are interesting, and I have never doubted the truth of this belief. So now I thought I'd put an interesting man to the test; I certainly wasn't going to accept his interestingness without proof.

The big question was: How was I going to make this interesting man show his mettle? Another fifteen minutes must have passed when I suddenly hit on a very simple and undoubtedly common stratagem; I simply dropped my handkerchief, and really the effect was breathtaking.

Not only did the interesting gentleman most gallantly (what else could he do?) pick my handkerchief up from the dirty floor; he also, of his own accord, took the opportunity to strike up a conversation.

"Well, young lady," he began affably, under his breath of course, because there was no need for the others to hear, "here is your property, but in exchange for your handkerchief I'd be glad to know your name."

Frankly I thought him rather bold, but since I was determined to be amused at all costs, I answered in the same tone and said: "Yes, sir, why not? My name is Miss Van Bergen."

He gave me a reproachful look and said ingratiatingly: "Oh, my dear young lady, I'd so much like to know your first name."

"Very well, it's Hetty."

"Oh, Hetty," my neighbor repeated, and then we chatted awhile about this and that, but for the life of me I couldn't make the conversation more interesting. I was expecting the man, who passed for interesting in the eyes of the world, to do that.

At the next station the gentleman got out, and I was terribly disappointed.

But then the old woman came out of her corner and started talking to me. She told me things that were so clever and interesting that the time flew and before I knew it I had arrived at my station.

I thanked the interesting little woman and now I know that the reputation of interesting men is based entirely on externals.

If you want to enjoy yourself on a trip or somewhere else, do what I did, try and find old and ugly people. They are much more likely to give you the entertainment you're looking for than gentlemen whose conceit is written all over their faces.

Why?

The little word "why" has been a very strong thing with me ever since I was a tiny little girl and couldn't even speak properly. It is a well-known fact that little children ask questions about everything because they are unfamiliar with everything. This was very much the case with me, but even when I grew older I couldn't wait to ask all kinds of questions, whether they could be answered or not. This is not so terrible in itself and I must say that my parents tried to answer every one of my questions very patiently, until . . . I began even badgering strangers, and *they* generally can't stand "children's endless questions." I must admit that this can be very tiresome, but I console myself with the idea that there is a saying that "you must ask in order to know," which couldn't be completely true, otherwise I'd be a professor by now.

When I grew older, I realized that it is not possible to ask every kind of question to everyone and that there are many "why's" that cannot be answered. I then followed from that that I tried to help myself by starting to think out these questions on my own. So I came to the important discovery that questions which one mustn't ask can be solved by oneself. Therefore, the little word "why" taught me not only to ask but to think.

Now as to the second part of the word "why." How would it be if everyone who did anything asked himself first, "Why?" I think they would then become more honest and much, much better people. For the best way to become honest and good is to keep examining oneself without stopping. I can imagine that the last thing people like to do is to confess to themselves their faults and their bad side (which everybody has). This is the case with children as well as grown-ups—in that respect I don't see any difference. Most people think parents should try to educate their children and see to it themselves that their characters develop as well as possible. This is certainly untrue. Children ought to educate themselves from their earliest youth and must try to show real character by themselves. Many will think this is crazy, but it isn't. Even a very small child is a little personality and has a conscience and should be brought up by being treated in this way, so that it will feel that its own conscience is punishing it in the harshest way possible. When children reach the age of fourteen or fifteen, every punishment is ridiculous. Such a child knows very well that no one, not even its own parents, can get anywhere with punishments and spankings. By arguing reasonably and by showing the child the mistakes it is making, one would get much better results than by strong punishments.

But here, I don't want to sound pedantic, but only to say that in the life of every child and every man, the little word "why" plays a big part, and rightly so. The saying, "You must ask in order to know," is true in so far as it leads to thinking about things, and by thinking nobody can ever get worse but will only get better.